THE
Blender Cocktail
BOOK

KENWOOD
Blender de luxe

THE
Blender Cocktail
BOOK

James McQuade
Marilyn Harvey

NEW YORK

Acknowledgments

The authors would like to express their appreciation
for the cooperation received from:
Atkinson, Baldwin & Co. Ltd.
Bennett Opie Ltd.
Bols Royal Distilleries
Finnish National Distillers Ltd.
S.F. & O. Hallgarten
Hedges & Butler Ltd.
James Burrough Ltd.
John Walker & Sons Ltd.
Martini & Rossi Ltd.
Matthew Clark & Sons Ltd.
Morgan Furze & Co. Ltd.
Saccone & Speed Ltd.
Seagram United Kingdom Ltd.
Tanqueray Gordon & Co. Ltd.
Thorn EMI Domestic Appliances Ltd. for the Kenwood Blenders
William Grant & Sons Ltd.

Photography by Derek Seaward

Photographic design by John Melville and James McQuade

Line illustrations by Robin Laurie

Cocktails shown on front cover
Left to right: *Blue Hawaiian, Easter Egg, Crystal Fizz,
Strawberry Daiquiri, Bloody Mary,
Peach Margarita, Bleu-Do-It.*

First published in USA 1984
by Exeter Books
Distributed by Bookthrift
Exeter is a trademark of Simon & Schuster
Bookthrift is a registered trademark of Simon & Schuster
New York, New York

Prepared by
Deans International Publishing
52–54 Southwark Street, London SE1 1UA
A division of The Hamlyn Publishing Group Limited
London·New York·Sydney·Toronto

ISBN 0–671–06910–1

Printed in Spain

Contents

Introduction

Until recently, cocktails were the preserve of professional cocktail bartenders who prepared their exquisite confections for those lucky enough to visit the top class establishments. Of course, many adventurous souls have dallied in the art of mixing drinks at home with some success but the traditional methods of preparation require special equipment which lies idle much of the time, making a home bar quite expensive and a cocktail something of a luxury. Now the use of the blender heralds a new era for cocktails. Most homes have a blender as standard kitchen equipment and making mixed drinks is a simple speedy operation that requires no particular skill or advance preparation, so mouthwatering mixtures bursting with colour, flavour and visual appeal can be produced in a matter of moments. The cocktail has entered the Age of Convenience and its revival in this thoroughly modern form means its growing acceptance as an integral part of entertainment and leisure.

Blended drinks add a special touch to home entertainment. A creamy concoction makes an excellent finale to a dinner party, unexpected guests can be made welcome with refreshing fruity mixtures, waistwatchers are able to whizz up light icy drinks, while trays of enticing cocktails are ready for thirsty party guests at the flick of a switch. Also, children are especially fond of the nutritious non-alcoholic drinks that can be made in the blender – a tall glass of frothing pink milk is pretty exciting stuff, especially if it has a straw in it! The blender has meant a change for some of the shaken and stirred drinks that are recognized as classics of the cocktail spectrum because the power of the machine amalgamates ingredients in a few seconds, yielding well chilled traditional-style cocktails with a minimum of effort and maximum effect. A few of these classics have also been expanded into families by the addition to the original recipes of fruits, dairy products or water ice, so producing some of the most popular of the modern cocktails.

Perhaps the most exciting aspect of using the blender to make mixed drinks is the enjoyment that comes from experimenting with recipes and the sense of satisfaction gained by presenting a guest with a delectable cocktail that is all your own handiwork. Happy mixing!

James McQuade and Marilyn Harvey

Left: *Cherry Silk*

What's in a Name!

There are almost as many legends explaining the origin of the word 'cocktail' as there are mixed drinks, and although most of them lean more towards fancy than fact, the very profusion of them shows that cocktails have been a source of inspiration to a considerable number of storytellers.

One of the more colourful explanations of the origin of the cocktail alleges that early Dutch settlers in the U.S.A. used to treat throat infections by painting the patient's throat with a cock's feather that had been dipped in strong spirit and home-made bitters. Perhaps some of the more adventurous patients gargled the mixture, which is likely to have numbed all sensation in the throat, with the result that spirit and bitters were drunk thereafter as a preventive medicine!

English gentlemen in the 18th century used to give their fighting cocks a potent concoction known as Cock Ale in the hope of improving their performance, then the spectators would toast the winning bird with a still more potent concoction, which had as many ingredients as the survivor had tail feathers, and it is likely that this drink also became known as cockale. Another of the more plausible explanations as to the origin of the word is that it is an Americanization of the French *coquetel* which was a mixed wine drink taken to America by Lafayette's soldiers when France supported the colonies in their revolution against Britain.

The best known legend is the one about King Axolotl VIII of Mexico who ruled in the early 1800s. The story goes that the American Army of the Southern States was involved in skirmishes with the Mexicans but the two leaders eventually met to discuss peace terms when a potentially volatile situation arose concerning who should drink first from the ceremonial gold cup. The cup was carried in by Coctel, the King's beautiful daughter who had mixed the drink herself and, realizing that one of the leaders would be insulted by drinking second, she drank the drink herself. It seems the American General announced that the diplomatic lady would be honoured by his Army – and so Coctel became Cocktail. Charming, but in point of fact the Gulf of Mexico was very much under the rule of Spain at that time, so the leaders were Spanish Viceroys and certainly not Indian Kings. Also, there is no trace of a King Axolotl VIII at any stage of Mexican history.

Mexico also features in another slightly more plausible story. English sailors, when in a Mexican port, would order a brandy or rum based mixture known as a 'drac', being a corruption of 'Drake', and the drink had to be stirred with a wooden spoon or stick. One particularly popular tavern used the slender smooth root of the *Cola de Gallo* plant as a stirrer and as this name translates into English as 'Cocktail' the drink eventually took on the same name, which was carried worldwide by the naval grapevine. There may be a glimmer of truth in the legend as it is still a practice in the West Indies to stir certain alcoholic drinks with a swizzle stick, which is the dried stem of a plant with a few smaller branches left on the end.

The first recorded reference to the word appears in 1802 in an American journal called *The Balance* which gives the following description: 'Cock tail, then, is a stimulating liquor, composed of spirits of any kind, sugar, water, and bitters – it is vulgarly called bittered sling and is supposed to be an excellent electioneering potion.' The consumption of cocktails was not limited to just election time either, as Charles Dickens made a note of their popularity in 1842 when he visited New York. He recorded that a Bitters was usually composed of brandy, gin or sherry mixed with various diffusions of herbs which stood in bottles on the counter of the bar.

Cocktails were well enough accepted in the U.S.A. by 1862 for a New York bartender, Jerry Thomas, to discuss them in depth in his book *The Bon Vivant's Guide or How to Mix Drinks*. He wrote: 'The cocktail is a modern invention and is generally used on fishing and sporting parties, although some patients insist that it is good in the morning as a tonic.' His cocktails were all served in a small bar glass and had names such as Fancy Brandy and Japanese. In England, bars serving cocktails were known as American Bars up until the 1950s, and one of the first of them is recorded as opening behind the Bank of England one hundred years earlier. Apparently an enterprising American felt there was money to be made selling Alabama Fog Cutters and Lightning Smashers to the City gents. By the 1930s even the French had taken note of the lure of the cocktail and in 1936 a Cocktail Cinema was a big success when it opened in Paris, with a five franc entrance fee that included one free cocktail.

Prohibition in the U.S.A. provided further impetus to the craze for mixed drinks as people added any number of weird ingredients to illegal firewater in an attempt to disguise the palate-stripping taste, so that by the time Prohibition was abolished the public had acquired a permanent liking for mixed drinks. The current boom began in the late Seventies, when long drinks with plenty of ice and fruit juices became popular, drinks such as Tequila Sunrise, Strawberry Daiquiri and Pina Colada. Today the short sharp drinks of pre-war times have been joined by their long sweet sisters, all answering to the name of cocktails.

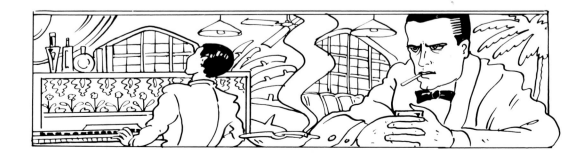

Toolkit

It takes only a few minutes to whizz up a tray of exciting cocktails that are guaranteed to turn any event into a celebration. Mixed drinks are fun to prepare and virtually no specialized equipment is absolutely necessary. Most homes have a blender or liquidizer in the kitchen and this is all that is needed to make the blended drinks in this book, and although a professional cocktail shaker is preferable, if one is not available, then a drink can easily be shaken in a cleaned large coffee jar. Virtually any jug can be used for stirring drinks as long as it is large enough to hold plenty of ice, while standard kitchen items such as strainers, spoons and glassware are perfectly adequate for mixing purposes. Most of the ingredients in these recipes are readily obtainable in good foodstores and many can be kept in the cupboard until required for a cocktail mixing session. Pages 13 to 15 show you how to use your equipment to the best effect.

The Blender

First time use

The first time a blender is used, it should be filled with warm water, the lid securely fitted in place and the machine switched on for 20–30 seconds. This removes any packaging dust and residual factory oils. Once dry, the blender is ready for use.

Do

Place the jug firmly on the base before switching on the machine.
Fit the lid securely before blending drinks as they may splash out of the jug.
Take care when drying by hand as the blade tips are sharp.
Blend for the time recommended in each recipe.
Wash the jug soon after using it as it is much easier to clean it before the residue crusts the inside surface.
Check the machine is positioned at Off before connecting to the power.

Cleaning

The simplest way to clean the blender after using it is to half fill the jug with warm water, switch on for 20–30 seconds, then empty this water out and rinse with clean warm water.

Don't

Remove the jug from the base while the blades are still spinning because this will damage the machine.
Be tempted to push the mixture down inside the jug while the blades are still spinning as this is very dangerous.
Leave items such as spoons or strainers inside the jug where they may be forgotten.
Pour boiling water into the blender jug.
Overfill the jug as this will severely reduce its capacity to operate efficiently.
Put a hand into the blender while it is working under any circumstances.

Scoop shows the amount of ice ideal for blending drinks.

A cocktail shaker should be two-thirds filled with ice before adding ingredients.

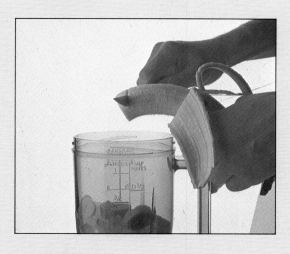

All fruit should be cut into cubes.

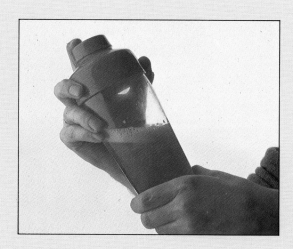

The shaker must be held firmly with both hands.

Blended fruit drinks should have a smooth creamy texture.

The ice can be held back by using the strainer provided in the shaker top.

The mixing glass should be half filled with ice before the ingredients are added to it.

A special strainer can be used to hold back the ice in the mixing glass. It is sometimes called a Hawthorn strainer and it allows the liquid to pour more easily.

The ice and ingredients should be stirred gently in a circular motion until the drink is sufficiently chilled.

Left to right: *Snowball, Bloody Mary, Brandy Crusta, Gibson, Frozen Medallion, Strawberry Colada, Pimms*

The ice can be held back by resting the barspoon on the pouring lip.

As the shaker is usually smaller than the mixing glass, the strainer can be held in position with one hand.

The flat end of the barspoon can be used for crushing sugar or mint.

Garnish

Garnish improves the appearance of most drinks and the word is used to refer to edible decoration. It can be either in the drink itself or placed on the side of the glass. In the illustration below, the Snowball is decorated with a cherry and a circle of orange held together by a cocktail stick, the Bloody Mary is complemented by a trimmed celery stick and the Brandy Crusta has a complete spiral of orange skin twisted around the inside of the glass. The Gibson has a single cocktail onion dropped to the bottom, the Frozen Medallion has a twist of lemon peel on top and the Strawberry Colada is decorated with a strawberry and wedge of pineapple on the side of the glass, while the Pimms has a sliver of cucumber skin and slices of citrus fruit submerged in the drink.

Ice

Ice, ice and more ice is the order of the day when it comes to preparing cocktails, for the time has gone when a drinker was happy with one ice cube swimming in lonely circles on top of a drink. Americans have always insisted on well iced drinks and the evolution of the modern American-style cocktail in Europe has meant an ice revolution as well.

Ice performs three very important functions when preparing cocktails. Firstly, it chills the liquid to an acceptable temperature. This is the major reason why drinks such as the Martini are stirred in a mixing glass, then strained off the ice. Secondly, it gives a blended drink more body and texture by thickening it and this is why so many recipes included in this book specify two ice cubes or one scoop of crushed ice. Thirdly, ice in a glass improves the appearance of a drink by giving it an extra dimension, removing the flat unexciting look so often noticeable when liquid is poured into a warm empty glass.

When mixing cocktails, always add the ice to the glass first and use plenty of it. It is the cheapest ingredient of a drink and if anything should go wrong with the preparation, then it can be disposed of without much waste. Also, it does not make sense to add the ice after the drink has been poured into the glass, not only because the ice is meant to chill the liquid, but because it is difficult to judge how much room to leave for the ice, so the drink may overflow if the cubes are added last.

Types of ice

Cubes These can be prepared in different sizes depending on the freezer tray, but the all-purpose cube is approximately 1 × 1 × 1½ in (2.5 × 2.5 × 5 cm) which is about 1 fl oz/30 ml of water. Cubes can be more quickly emptied from the hard plastic trays rather than from the rubber trays or soft plastic ones on the market.
Blocks Large blocks of ice can be purchased from ice suppliers and are very useful for parties. They can be kept in buckets or bins to chill minerals, beer or wine bottles, and pieces chipped off a large block are suitable for cooling champagne in an ice bucket. Be careful when ordering this sort of ice to specify what it is for, as ice slabs used to cool fish have a salt water content and are not made with drinking water.
Crushed ice Ice cubes can be crushed by wrapping them in a clean tea towel and hitting them with a rolling pin or meat hammer. However, inexpensive hand-operated ice crushers are readily available, and for parties an electric ice crusher provides a steady stream of fine ice.

Preparing ice

Ice that is on the point of melting is of little use in a drink. The best way to ensure that there is a supply of hard dry ice cubes is to spend a little time preparing them in advance. Tip the cubes out of their trays and into a plastic container which can fit into the freezer compartment. Once they have been in the freezer for half an hour, shuffle them around in the plastic container to make sure they are not sticking together. Crushed ice can be treated in a similar manner. For parties, ice can be obtained in quantity from most supermarkets and outlets that sell liquor.

Left to right: *Chilled Vodka, Chilled Champagne*

Ingredients

Bitters Angostura bitters come in a quarter bottle size and one will last for a very long time as recipes only stipulate a few drops of it. This is because it is a concentrated essence with an alcoholic base. It has a special pourer to regulate the flow rate and the top needs to be wiped well to prevent it becoming sticky.

Coconut cream This is available in cans in most good supermarkets. Once opened, tip the whole contents into the blender and turn it on for a few seconds to amalgamate the solids and oils. It can be then stored in a plastic container and refrigerated for a few weeks. It has a powerful coconut flavour, so small measures of it will achieve the desired result. Do not use creamed coconut, which is available in packets, or coconut oil for mixing drinks.

Consommé Cans of beef consommé or bouillon are used for Bullshots.

Cream Fresh cream is used in many recipes, especially those suitable for after dinner drinking. It is essential that the cream be free flowing and very fresh, and double cream (U.S. heavy cream) is best. Cream tends to mask other flavours and make too sickly a drink if not used in the correct proportion. Drinks such as the Alexander and Golden Cadillac require cream to be added to the drink, and others such as the Envy and the Irish Coffee have it floated on top.

Egg white Egg white is an ingredient in many cocktails as it adds body and life to the presentation. Only a dash of it is required and one egg white is enough to make about three drinks. Put the egg white into a small jug and cut it thoroughly with a knife. This will allow it to pour freely without coming out all in a blob. Do not store unused egg white as it is quickly contaminated.

Grenadine This is a reddish pink coloured sugar syrup, flavoured with pomegranates. It is non-alcoholic and is used in cocktails to provide colour interest and sweetening. It livens up non-alcoholic mixtures, and children find it exciting to have pink drinks, especially those who are not too keen on plain milk.

Ice cream   Ice cream is being used more frequently as it is an ideal ingredient for blended drinks. As it is already cold, ice blocks are not necessary, so ice cream drinks are useful when caught unawares by visitors. They also make an interesting alternative to a sweet at the end of a meal.

Juices   Fresh juices make the most interesting cocktails and an electric juice squeezer makes light work of preparing them. However, cartons of orange, pineapple and grapefruit juices are very suitable substitutes and these can be stored for a few days once opened. It is strongly recommended that lemon and lime juices be freshly squeezed as the fresh fruity acid flavour cannot be gained from bottled or canned juices.

Minerals   Many of the long drink recipes require minerals, the most frequently used being soda, tonic, dry ginger ale, lemonade and cola. These can be stored in a cupboard for a few months or a mineral maker can produce these drinks quickly and cheaply.

Sugar syrup   This is ready-made sugar syrup sold by the bottle in most outlets that sell liquor. It is used to sweeten drinks as sugar crystals would make a drink gritty to taste. It can easily be made at home by slowly dissolving 3 cups of sugar in 1 cup of water, then boiling the mixture for a few minutes. This syrup may be stored indefinitely.

Syrups   Other non-alcoholic syrups useful for cocktail making are orgeat which has an almond flavour, fraise which is strawberry and cassis which is blackcurrant.

Other kitchen supplies

demerara sugar	olives
caster (U.S.	coffee beans
superfine) sugar	Worcestershire sauce
cube sugar	Tabasco sauce
pearl onions	nutmeg
maraschino cherries	celery salt
	salt and pepper

Fruit

Fruit and the blender make an excellent partnership when preparing mixed drinks, as the machine makes fast work of reducing the fruit to the consistency of a purée which, in turn, gives texture and substance to the drink. Some fruits require a little extra attention before they can be blended, but the time it takes to prepare them is amply rewarded by a cocktail with plenty of colour, body and flavour. Following are the fruits that most lend themselves to being blended, and where appropriate a spirit, liqueur or syrup with a similar flavour is mentioned, as they are often used in combination with fruits to heighten the taste.

Apples Any eating apple is suited to the blender but it must be peeled and cored first. Calvados is a spirit distilled from apples, so recipes such as the Apple Daiquiri use both apples and spirit together to achieve a clean refreshing flavour.

Apricots The flesh of the apricot is firm but juicy when it is properly ripe. If fresh apricots are not available, the canned fruit is quite suitable once it has been well drained.

Avocados Avocado pears are actually a fruit, although they are more often treated as a vegetable. Ripe avocado flesh blends particularly well with dairy products to produce luscious thick-textured drinks that are almost a meal in themselves.

Bananas The soft texture of a ripe banana is especially suited to the blender, and as the natural flavour of the fruit is very strong, the drink takes on an assertive banana taste. A dash of crème de banane will sweeten a cocktail made with banana. It is important to blend the drink until it is smooth, otherwise pieces of fruit will clog the straw.

Cherries Canned pitted cherries may be used in blended drinks. They are preferable to fresh cherries as the stones have already been removed and long soaking in the syrup softens the skins. Cherry brandy, kirsch and maraschino can all be used to reinforce the cherry flavour and maraschino cherries are sold ready bottled for use as cocktail decoration.

Grapefruit Grapefruit juice features in many recipes because its assertive citrus tang adds character to drinks. Unsweetened fresh grapefruit juice in cartons has an authentic flavour and can be refrigerated for a few days.

Lemon The lemon is the workhorse fruit of the cocktail industry because it is inexpensive, readily available and has a high acid content that balances the sugar level of alcoholic beverages such as liqueurs. Fresh lemon juice is infinitely superior to any bottled or packaged product.

Limes Fresh lime juice has a unique sweet-sour taste that is unequalled as a palate freshener and it is worth going to some trouble to obtain limes for recipes that specify them. Lime cordial is used in a range of mixed drinks which intend it to sweeten as well as flavour a mixture. A slice of lime in a simple gin and tonic and a used lime shell in a Moscow Mule both contribute the concentrated oils contained in the skin to the drinks.

Mandarin A ripe mandarin or similar orange has the advantage of being very juicy, yet less aggressively citrus in flavour, so some recipes use the segments and may even underline the taste by adding a mandarin liqueur.

Mango The bright orange-yellow flesh and the distinctive aroma of a mango add colour, flavour and an exotic aspect to a mixed drink. Fresh mango must be very ripe, so canned mango is a very acceptable substitute. Mango nectar provides the fruit flavour, but will not give a drink the same thickened texture achieved by blending the fruit itself.

Melon Melon flesh adds body to a drink but it has a subdued flavour once it has been blended with liquid, so liqueurs such as Midori Melon Liqueur are often used to bolster the taste of the drink.

Orange The orange is the most popular of citrus fruits and the unsweetened juice is readily available in cartons, although freshly squeezed juice adds much more piquancy to a cocktail, especially if the recipe only contains a few ingredients. Pieces of orange can be blended whole and sometimes even the skin is added, so in these cases it is best to choose a thin-skinned variety of the fruit. Dry Orange Curacao is an excellent choice from the wide range of orange liqueurs that may accompany the fresh fruit flavour.

Passionfruit These small tropical fruits are full of very sweet flesh and black seeds. The freshly squeezed fruit can be added to blended recipes, although bottled passionfruit nectar achieves much the same effect.

Peaches Ripe peaches have soft sweet flesh that is easily parted from the stone. They make delicious mixed drinks, but must be peeled before going into the blender. Drained canned peaches are quite suitable, although not as much sweetener is necessary as they have been soaked in syrup, and bottled peach nectar is very effective at flavouring a drink.

Pears Most varieties of pear are suitable for blending purposes once they have been peeled, but they bruise easily and should be handled with care. Drained canned pears are an acceptable substitute and they marry well with poire Williams liqueur.

Pineapple A ripe pineapple is absolutely laden with sweet juice which makes excellent blended mixed drinks. Canned slices or cubes can be used quite successfully even though they do not have the heightened flavour of the fresh fruit. Pineapple juice is an ingredient in many modern cocktails and the unsweetened cartons can be refrigerated for a few days.

Raspberries Fully ripe raspberries contribute a sharp tangy bite to a blended drink as well as an appetizing colour. Raspberries can be frozen and the blended purée will keep under refrigeration for a few days. A raspberry liqueur or syrup, usually sold under the name Framboise, will add any touch of sweetness necessary for these drinks.

Strawberries The ever popular strawberry brings colour and piquancy to a fruit cocktail, but strawberries should be well washed to avoid a gritty taste. The Strawberry Daiquiri is one of the most famous modern cocktails and it shows how successfully fresh strawberries and strawberry syrup, known as Fraise, combine in a drink.

Glassware

The glass is an essential part of the presentation of any drink and is as important as any of the ingredients or decoration. The right glass will enhance the appearance, the wrong glass will ruin it. For example, champagne from a beer glass just doesn't have the same effect as from a slim elegant flute glass. An excellent range of modern glassware is now readily available, and some styles can be used for many types of drinks. A glass should have a stable base that is not easily upset as a spilt cocktail has disastrous effects on upholstery, carpet and guests' clothing. Stemmed glassware allows a drink to remain cold to the last drop, so a stem not only highlights the elegant appearance but has the practical function of keeping warm hands away from the drink. Another advantage of a stem is that it allows any condensation to stay on the outside of the bowl of the glass.

Glassware must be kept clean for health reasons and a dirty glass also dulls the visual presentation. Glasses should be washed separately from plates and cutlery to avoid grease stains and it is best to polish a glass with a dry glass cloth prior to using it as this will guarantee a clean dry shiny piece of equipment. It is dangerous to wipe glassware with a damp cloth as it will stick to the glass which is likely to break – the stem is especially vulnerable in this respect – while a damp glass detracts from a drink containing carbonated ingredients such as beer, ginger ale or champagne by appearing to 'flatten' the drink.

Store glasses in a dust-free place that is out of the reach of children. They are best kept upright in a cupboard as a glass that rests on a shelf rim downwards for too long will develop a stale musty smell that can permeate the flavour of a drink. A cocktail in a well chosen glass is a pretty sight that only needs a little decoration to set it off. It also looks attractive to offer the drink on a tray which makes it easier for the guest to take it, while ensuring that he or she appreciates its visual appeal. The illustrations in this book show good examples of glasses which are suitable for blended cocktails and will withstand the wear and tear of frequent use, while each recipe mentions the size of glass which is best suited to that particular drink.

Glass styles

Cocktail glass This is the classic V-shaped stemmed glass which holds 3–4 fl oz/90–120 ml. It is best in clear glass as the drink is then the highlight of the presentation. Coloured stems are very popular but restrict the colours of cocktails. A green drink in a purple stemmed glass does not have much to recommend it.

Double Cocktail glass This may have a V-shaped or curved bowl and holds 6–7 fl oz/175–200 ml. It is particularly useful for frappés and blended drinks.

Goblet The stemmed glass known as the Paris goblet is an excellent all-purpose glass. It suits hot drinks, beers and blended drinks.

Highball The large straight-sided tumbler is known as a highball glass as it was first used to serve Highballs. Now it is also the glass for long drinks requiring ice and holds 8–12 fl oz/225–350 ml. This style of glass lends itself to decoration with stirrers, straws and slices of fruit.

Old-fashioned This is a short straight-sided tumbler which takes its name from the drink known as an Old Fashioned. Its use is for spirits served over ice or for short drinks poured unstrained into a glass.

Flute This long tapering elegant glass is the classic shape for champagne as the bubbles are able to rise in a continuous stream from the narrow bottom.

Saucer glass The saucer-shaped bowl is suitable for cream or ice cream based drinks but not for champagne drinks as it does not have enough depth to allow the bubbles to rise sufficiently.

Hot Drinks glass   Some glasses are designed specifically for hot drinks as they have a handle and a short stem. They should be made of heat resistant glass to be of real use and drinks such as the Irish Coffee look effective in them.

Liqueur glass   The small stemmed glass suitable for a measure of liqueur holds 1–2½ fl oz/30–75 ml of liquid. This style is also used for serving aquavit or schnapps.

Sundae glass   The classic ice cream sundae glass consists of a long tapering bowl with a flaired edge and is mounted on a small stem. Blended drinks look particularly effective in them.

Sherry glass   The small tulip-shaped bowl is especially designed for sherry or port and is sometimes known as a copita. It is also ideal for brandy and large measures of a liqueur.

Tiki glass   This is a large glass bowl with a Polynesian face mounted on a short stem. Tiki glasses suit icy fruit-based drinks as they have a large capacity.

Tulip glass   This elongated bowl glass is usually used for wine service but also makes an excellent cocktail glass.

Novelty containers

Coconut shell   To make a coconut shell ready for use as a container, saw the top third off and remove enough shell from the bottom to make a stable base. Then remove all trace of coconut flesh from inside the shell.

Ogen melon   These are effective on a 'one-off' basis for a drink and are prepared by cutting off a top section and hollowing out the majority of the flesh.

Pineapple shell   The lower two thirds of a pineapple makes an unusual container as a glass is slipped inside to take the drink. Hollow out the pineapple by placing a straight-sided glass rim downwards and pushing it through the flesh. Then slip a sharp slim-bladed knife through the skin and work it back and forth to cut the flesh across just below the rim of the glass. The glass shaped 'core' can then be extracted with the glass. The shell must be kept in the freezer until required for health reasons and a fresh glass should be inserted for every drink.

Wooden bowls   These are excellent containers for the Polynesian-style drinks and often each bowl holds two or more drinks, being presented with a long straw for each person.

Measures

The most important point to remember when measuring liquids is that a drink only tastes as it should when mixed in the correct proportions. For example, when a recipe calls for equal parts of gin, Cointreau and lemon juice, then equal amounts of the three ingredients must be mixed together. If the host decides to be particularly generous and adds more gin than Cointreau or lemon juice, then the drink is out of balance and will taste that way, so the drinker is likely to wonder why the host was so proud of his cocktail mixing ability.

The recipes in this book have been written in measures (abbreviated as ms), so it is possible to use the same recipe to make just one drink or multiples of it. The mixer should decide just how much volume his measure will be – it may be an ounce, a cup or even a bottle – as long as the same measuring instrument is used for all ingredients, then the recipe will provide a well balanced drink. A bottle cap, an egg cup, liqueur glass or even a small coffee cup will all serve as measures, but it is best to become accustomed to the one utensil so that a known quantity of drink is prepared every time.

Measures and glasses – equivalent capacities

(Table to two points of decimals)

Centilitres (cl)	U.K. fluid ounces (fl oz)	U.S.A. liquid or fluid ounces (lq oz)	Remarks
0.1	0.03	0.03	Dash = 5 drops
0.5	0.18	0.17	Teaspoon = $\frac{1}{8}$ fl oz
			Dessertspoon = $\frac{1}{4}$ fl oz
1	0.35	0.34	Tablespoon = $\frac{1}{2}$ fl oz
2	0.70	0.68	6-out measure = $\frac{5}{6}$ fl oz
			5-out measure = 1 fl oz
3	1.06	1.01	4-out measure = $1\frac{1}{4}$ fl oz
4	1.40	1.35	Pony (U.S.A.) = 1 fl oz (approx.)
5	1.76	1.69	Jigger (U.S.A.) = $1\frac{1}{2}$ fl oz (approx.)
6	2.11	2.03	
7	2.46	2.37	Cocktail glasses vary from 2 to $3\frac{1}{2}$ oz.
8	2.82	2.71	$2\frac{1}{2}$ oz is an average U.K. size
9	3.17	3.04	
10	3.52	3.38	
11	3.87	3.72	
12	4.22	4.06	4-oz wine glass (U.S.A.); a good size for
13	4.58	4.40	Sours, like vodka and tomato juice.
14	4.93	4.73	A U.K. size is a 5-oz wine glass.
15	5.28	5.07	14.2 cl = 5 fl oz = 1 Gill or Noggin
16	5.63	5.41	
17	5.98	5.75	
18	6.34	6.09	
19	6.69	6.42	
20	7.04	6.77	
21	7.39	7.10	
22	7.74	7.44	
23	8.10	7.78	23 cl = U.K. 8-oz wine glass
24	8.45	8.12	
25	8.80	8.45	
26	9.15	8.80	
27	9.50	9.13	
28	9.85	9.47	28.4 cl = 10 fl oz = U.K. half-pint.
29	10.21	9.81	Tumblers can be smaller, but 10 oz gives wider scope
30	10.56	10.14	33 cl = 12-oz wine glass
50	17.60	16.91	56 cl = U.K. pint
75	26.40	25.36	75 cl = One 'Reputed' Quart = usual wine bottle
100	35.20	33.81	100 cl = 1 litre

1.14 litres = 40 fl oz = 8.0 gills = One Imperial Quart = $\frac{1}{4}$ Imperial Gallon.

BRANDY: *the French Connection*

Brandy is the spirit that results from distilling wine, and although many countries now produce brandy it originated in France and the best still comes from there. Cognac is a town near the western seaboard of France, and in Roman times the good citizens of Cognac learned two skills from their Imperial masters – to extract salt from seawater and make wine from grapes. Salt was a most precious commodity as a flavouring and preservative, so the area prospered over the centuries because the Dutch sea traders came for the salt and took the wine as well. It was not particularly good wine, travel affected it and the casks took up much needed space on board ship, so the practical French decided to boil it down. This reduced its bulk considerably, raised the alcohol content which strengthened the wine and lowered the amount of taxation the traders had to pay, as this was determined by bulk. It had an unusual taste as it was now a concentrated essence, and the Dutch referred to it as *brandewijn* which means 'burnt wine'. The intention was that this concentrate would be diluted with water once it reached its destination, but customers found they actually liked the taste better without water, so began asking for 'brandy'. As the brandy from the Cognac area became more popular production techniques were improved, and during the 18th century enterprising young British businessmen began their own firms in the area, which is why some cognacs today carry names such as Martell, Hine, Hennessy and Delamain.

As brandy can be distilled from any grapes, it was not long before other areas of France as well as other countries began producing brandy. However, cognac comes only from around the French town of that name, so that although cognac is a brandy, not all brandy is cognac. Brandy improves with age in casks before being bottled and sold, resulting in a wide price range for the spirit as it is very expensive to hold stock at the distillery while it ages. Good standard cognac often carries three stars or the initials V.S. on the label which means it is about a year and a half old, and these are eminently suitable for mixing cocktails. Four-year-old cognac carries the letters V.S.O.P. meaning Very Special Old Pale and cognac over five years may be labelled Extra or Napoleon – these cognacs are best drunk neat to appreciate their style and finesse. Some Houses market a luxury cognac that has been aged in cask for many years before being released for sale, usually in exquisite packaging to highlight the quality of the spirit. Hennessy's Paradis, for example, is blended from cognacs over fifty years old, and the Remy Martin Louis XIII is marketed in a crystal Baccarat decanter. Price determines that such cognacs be offered to those guests who recognize a goodly nip of brandy when they taste one.

Europeans are quite partial to fruit brandy and seem to drink it at any hour. It is poured into morning coffee, tea cakes are drenched in it and after dinner it is sipped neat to help digestion and add to the general feeling of well being that follows a good meal. The spirit is made by steeping fruits such as cherries, pears and raspberries in alcohol, then distilling the mixture. The result is a brilliantly clear liquid with the rich scent of fruit and a strong dry flavour. A fruit spirit is often called an eau-de-vie and the best of them come from that part of Europe covering Switzerland, Germany's Black Forest and French Alsace, as this is where summer fruit grows in abundance in the rich soil that also provides some of Europe's finest pastures. Some of the best known producers are Schladerer from Germany, Dettling from Switzerland and Trimbach from France.

Frozen Classics

Alexanders

The Alexander is the most famous of the cream cocktails. It has always had brandy as its spirit ingredient, although in the United States it is recognized as a gin-based drink. However, the combination of gin, brown crème de cacao and cream was called the 'Princess Mary' by Harry McElhone who created it whilst working in Nice, to celebrate the Princess's marriage to Lord Lascelles in 1922, so it would appear that the drink experienced a change of name once it crossed the Atlantic. By substituting ice cream for cream, this cocktail takes on the thick velvety texture that is so suitable for slow sipping enjoyment.

Brandy Alexander

1 ms brandy
1 ms Bols brown Crème de Cacao
1 ms cream
2 dashes nutmeg

Shake all the ingredients except the nutmeg with ice and strain into a cocktail glass or small goblet. Dust nutmeg on top.

Frozen Alexander

1 ms brandy
1 ms Bols brown Crème de Cacao
1 small scoop vanilla ice cream
flaked chocolate

Blend together all except the chocolate on slow speed until smooth, then pour into a small glass. Sprinkle chocolate on top.

Strawberry Alexander

1 ms brandy
1 ms Bols white Crème de Cacao
1 small scoop strawberry ice cream
1 strawberry

Blend all the ingredients together on slow speed until smooth, then pour into a small glass.

Cadillacs

The Golden Cadillac was invented in the United States during the car-mad Sixties, where it was used to promote the liqueur Galliano that was enjoying a meteoric rise to fame, thanks to the mythical Mr. Harvey Wallbanger. This sophisticated blend of flavours, named after the American ideal of mechanized luxury, has become a modern classic because it successfully combines liqueurs and cream without the need for a spirit base.

Left to right: *Raspberry Daiquiri, Pina Colada, Golden Cadillac, Melon Daiquiri*

Golden Cadillac

(Illustrated on page 31)

1 ms Galliano
1 ms Bols white Crème de Cacao
1 ms cream

Shake all the ingredients together with ice and strain into a cocktail glass.

Orange Cadillac

1 ms Galliano
1 ms Bols white Crème de Cacao
1 ms orange juice
1 ms cream
1 scoop crushed ice

Blend all the ingredients together on fast speed for 10 seconds, then pour into a small goblet. Serve with short straws.

Silver Cadillac

1 ms Galliano
1 ms Bols white Crème de Cacao
1 small scoop vanilla ice cream

Blend all the ingredients together on slow speed until smooth, then pour into a small goblet.

Daiquiris

The Daiquiri has been adapted to a sorbet-style fruity drink, whizzed up in the blender. There is a whole family of these concoctions, the most popular being the strawberry.

The elegant short drink so popular in the first cocktail era is now often referred to as a Lime Daiquiri, although its tangy thirst-quenching flavour still ensures its position as a cocktail classic. It takes its name from the Daiquiri iron mines in Cuba, where American advisers became particularly fond of the local brew of rum, sugar and fresh lime juice which was served to the workers after they emerged from the pits. The secret of the modern Daiquiri is to highlight the fruit by adding a dash of the appropriate liqueur and blending the mixture with plenty of crushed ice until it has the correct texture.

The Daiquiri

$1\frac{1}{2}$ ms light rum
$\frac{1}{2}$ ms fresh lime juice
$\frac{1}{4}$ ms sugar syrup

Shake all the ingredients with ice and strain into a cocktail glass.

Coconut Daiquiri

1 ms Malibu coconut liqueur
$\frac{1}{2}$ ms light rum
$\frac{1}{4}$ ms fresh lime juice
1 dash egg white

Shake all the ingredients with ice and strain into a cocktail glass.

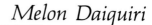

Frozen Daiquiri

1½ ms light rum
¼ ms fresh lime juice
¼ ms Bols Maraschino Liqueur
1 dash sugar syrup
2 scoops crushed ice

Blend all the ingredients together on fast speed for 5 seconds, then pour into a small goblet. Serve with short straws.

Apple Daiquiri

1 ms light rum
1 ms calvados
½ ms fresh lime juice
¼ peeled apple
2 dashes sugar syrup
1 scoop crushed ice

Blend all the ingredients together on slow speed for 15 seconds, then pour into a medium-size glass and decorate with a slice of apple or a grape. Serve with short straws.

Banana Daiquiri

1½ ms light rum or 1 ms banana rum
½ ms fresh lime juice
½ ms Bols Crème de Banane
¼ banana
½ scoop crushed ice

Blend all the ingredients together on slow speed for 10 seconds, then pour into a bowl-type glass. Decorate with a slice of lime and a red cherry. Serve with short straws.

Melon Daiquiri

(Illustrated on page 31)

1 ms light rum
½ ms Midori Melon Liqueur
½ ms fresh lime juice
2 dashes sugar syrup
4 pieces diced melon
1 scoop crushed ice

Blend all the ingredients together on slow speed for 7 seconds, then pour into a sundae glass. Decorate with diced melon and an orange cocktail cherry. Sprinkle ground ginger on top. Serve with short straws.

Peach Daiquiri

1 ms light rum
½ ms Bols Peach Brandy
½ ms fresh lime juice
2 halves of canned peaches
¼ scoop crushed ice

Blend all the ingredients together on medium speed until the texture is smooth, then pour into a double cocktail glass. Decorate with slices of peach and serve with short straws.

Raspberry Daiquiri

(Illustrated on page 31)

1½ ms light rum
½ ms raspberry syrup
½ ms fresh lime juice
6 raspberries
1 scoop crushed ice

Blend all the ingredients together on slow speed for 3 seconds, then on medium for 2 seconds and finally on fast speed for 5 seconds. Pour into a large goblet and serve with short straws.

33

Sherbert Daiquiri

$1\frac{1}{2}$ ms light rum
$\frac{1}{2}$ ms Bols Dry Orange Curacao
$\frac{1}{2}$ ms fresh lime juice
$\frac{1}{2}$ ms orange juice
1 scoop crushed ice

Blend all the ingredients together on fast speed for 7 seconds, then pour into a tall glass. Decorate with a sprig of mint and serve with long straws.

Left to right: *Vodka Freeze, Silver Fizz, Chocolate Finger Fizz, Crimson Fizz, Margarita, Blue Hawaiian*

Strawberry Daiquiri

(Illustrated on front cover)

$1\frac{1}{2}$ ms light rum
$\frac{1}{2}$ ms strawberry syrup
$\frac{1}{2}$ ms fresh lime juice
4 strawberries
1 scoop crushed ice

Blend all the ingredients together on slow speed for 5 seconds, then on medium speed for 3 seconds. Pour into a bowl or long glass. Decorate with a strawberry and serve with straws.

Fizzes

The Fizz is a small drink that consists of spirit, fruit juice and powdered sugar which are shaken together until as cold as possible, then strained into the glass and topped with carbonated water which creates the fizz. It is traditionally a morning drink and is meant to be consumed fairly quickly, while the bubbles are still in the glass. The addition of egg adds to the texture and appearance, whilst the blender makes it much easier to thoroughly amalgamate and chill the base ingredients. Several of the well known variations, such as the New Orleans Fizz, contain cream and it is a short step to the use of ice cream to create a range of ultra-modern fizzes.

Gin Fizz

1½ ms dry gin
½ ms fresh lemon juice
1 teaspoon powdered sugar
soda water

Shake all the ingredients except the soda water with ice until very cold. Strain into an 8-oz/225-ml goblet and top up with soda water, stirring as you do so. Decorate with a slice of lemon.

The above ingredients can easily be adapted for blending by simply adding two or three ice cubes to the recipe and blending on slow speed for 10 seconds, then pouring into a medium-size goblet before topping up with soda water.

Golden Fizz

Same as Gin Fizz, with the addition of an egg yolk.

Jackhammer Fizz

Same as Gin Fizz, except use Jack Daniels instead of gin.

Pink Lady Fizz

Same as Gin Fizz, except use grenadine instead of sugar.

Royal Fizz

Same as Gin Fizz, with the addition of a whole egg.

Silver Fizz

Illustrated on pages 34–35)

Same as Gin Fizz, with the addition of an egg white.

Texas Fizz

Same as Gin Fizz, with the addition of 1 teaspoon grenadine and 1 ms orange juice.

Chocolate Finger Fizz

(Illustrated on pages 34–35)

1 ms light rum
½ ms Bols Chocolate Mint
1 dash Bols green Crème de Menthe
1 dash fresh lemon juice
1 scoop chocolate ice cream
soda water

Blend together all except the soda water on slow speed for 10 seconds, then pour into a large goblet. Splash in soda water and serve with a chocolate flake and straws.

Crimson Fizz

(Illustrated on pages 34–35)

1 ms gin
1 ms fresh lemon juice
2 dashes strawberry syrup
6 strawberries
soda water

Blend together all except the soda water on slow speed for 5 seconds, then on medium speed for 3 seconds and finally on high speed for 3 seconds. Pour into a tall glass filled with ice, top up with soda water and serve with straws.

Morning Fizz

1 ms vodka
3 ms grapefruit juice
½ ms sugar syrup
1 scoop crushed ice
1 ms soda water

Blend together all except the soda water on fast speed for 7 seconds, then pour into a 6-oz/175-ml goblet and top up with soda water. Decorate with a slice of lime and a red cherry.

New Orleans Fizz

2 ms gin
½ ms fresh lime juice
½ ms fresh lemon juice
2 dashes sugar syrup
3 dashes orange flower water
2 teaspoons cream
½ ms soda water
1 scoop crushed ice

Blend all the ingredients together, including the soda water, on fast speed for 10 seconds, then pour into a small highball glass. Serve with straws.

Pineapple Fizz

1 ms light rum
1 ms golden rum
2 ms pineapple juice
1 teaspoon sugar syrup
1 ms lemonade
1 scoop crushed ice

Blend all the ingredients together, including the lemonade, for 10 seconds, then pour into a highball glass or pineapple shell. Splash in extra lemonade and serve with straws.

Ramos Chill Fizz

2 ms gin
1 ms fresh lemon juice
1 ms Bols Dry Orange Curacao
1 scoop vanilla ice cream
soda water

Blend together all except the soda water on slow speed for 15 seconds, then pour into a tall glass and top up with soda water. Serve with long straws.

Margaritas

The Margarita has become identified as the national drink of Mexico because of its tequila base. Traditionally, a Margarita is served in a glass which has been rimmed with salt, so that the chilled and flavoured tequila can be sipped through it. However, Margarita has remained a thoroughly fashionable lady by adapting very well to preparation in the blender, and the addition of fruit and an appropriate liqueur creates the popular modern version.

The Margarita

(Illustrated on pages 34–35)

1 ms tequila
1 ms triple sec
1 ms fresh lime juice

Rub the rim of the glass with a slice of lemon or lime, then dip into fine salt. Shake all the ingredients with ice and strain into a prepared glass.

Strawberry Margarita

2 ms tequila
1 ms fresh lime juice
1 ms triple sec
3 strawberries
2 dashes strawberry syrup
1 scoop crushed ice

Blend all the ingredients together on slow speed for 5 seconds, then on medium speed for 3 seconds. Pour into a medium-size glass and serve with straws.

Other fruit Margaritas can be enjoyed by substituting the fruit and using the appropriate liqueur or syrup.

Peach Margarita

(Illustrated on front cover)

$1\frac{1}{2}$ ms tequila
1 ms fresh lime juice
$\frac{1}{2}$ ms Bols Peach Brandy
1 half peach
1 scoop crushed ice

Blend all the ingredients together on medium speed until smooth, then pour into a medium-size glass and serve with straws.

Frozen Margarita

2 ms tequila
1 ms fresh lime juice
1 ms triple sec
1 scoop orange sorbet

Blend all the ingredients together on slow speed for 10 seconds, then pour into a small goblet. Decorate with a slice of lime and serve with straws.

Chiquita

1 ms tequila
1 ms triple sec
1 ms fresh lime juice
4 pitted cherries
1 scoop crushed ice

Blend all the ingredients together on slow speed for 15 seconds, then pour into a medium-size glass. Serve with short straws.

Pina Coladas

The name Pina Colada means crushed pineapple and this is the fruit ingredient of the drink that revolutionized the cocktail industry by showing how well it could be made in the blender. Long icy drinks with plenty of flavour are being demanded by today's cocktail drinkers, and this pineapple-coconut combination is top favourite. Already there is a range of blended variations to this modern classic.

Banana Colada

$1\frac{1}{2}$ ms golden rum
$\frac{1}{2}$ ms coconut cream
$\frac{1}{2}$ ms Bols Crème de Banane
2 ms pineapple juice
$\frac{1}{2}$ banana
1 scoop crushed ice

Blend all the ingredients together on slow speed for 7 seconds, then on fast speed until smooth. Pour into a medium-size glass and serve with straws.

Blue Hawaiian

(Illustrated on page 35)

$1\frac{1}{2}$ ms light rum
$\frac{1}{2}$ ms Bols Blue Curacao
$\frac{1}{2}$ ms coconut cream
2 ms pineapple juice
1 scoop crushed ice

Blend all the ingredients together on fast speed for 7 seconds, then pour into a medium-size glass. Decorate with a wedge of pineapple and a red cocktail cherry. Serve with straws.

Casablanca

1½ ms light rum
½ ms coconut cream
2 ms pineapple juice
½ ms grenadine
1 scoop crushed ice

Blend all the ingredients together on fast speed for 7 seconds, then pour into a medium-size glass. Decorate with a wedge of pineapple and a green cocktail cherry. Serve with straws.

Chi Chi

1½ ms vodka
½ ms coconut cream
2 ms pineapple juice
1 scoop crushed ice

Blend all the ingredients together on fast speed for 7 seconds, then pour into a medium-size glass. Decorate with a wedge of pineapple and a red cocktail cherry. Serve with straws.

Happy Jack

1½ ms calvados
½ ms coconut cream
2 ms pineapple juice
1 scoop crushed ice

Blend all the ingredients together on fast speed for 7 seconds, then pour into a medium-size glass. Decorate with a wedge of pineapple and a spiral of apple skin. Serve with straws.

Coco Colada

1 ms dark rum
1 ms Bols brown Creme de Cacao
2 ms pineapple juice
½ ms coconut cream
2 scoops crushed ice

Blend all the ingredients together on slow speed for 10 seconds, then pour into a large bowl glass. Sprinkle cocoa powder on top and serve with straws.

Pina Colada

(Illustrated on page 31)

1½ ms light rum
½ ms coconut cream
2 ms pineapple juice
1 scoop crushed ice

Blend all the ingredients together on fast speed for 7 seconds, then pour into a medium-size glass. Decorate with a wedge of pineapple and orange cocktail cherries. Serve with straws.

Strawberry Colada

(Illustrated on page 15)

1½ ms golden rum
½ ms coconut cream
2 ms pineapple juice
½ ms strawberry syrup
4 strawberries
1 scoop crushed ice

Blend all the ingredients together on medium speed until smooth, then pour into a medium-size glass. Decorate with a wedge of pineapple and a strawberry. Serve with straws.

Screwdrivers

The Screwdriver is one of the world's simplest drinks. Folklore has it that it was invented by oil rig workers in the Middle East who slaked their thirst with vodka and orange juice, then used a screwdriver to mix the drink together. Some interesting variations can be quickly prepared by blending orange-flavoured water ice and liqueurs.

Screwdriver

1 ms vodka
4 ms orange juice

Fill a tall glass with ice, then add the ingredients. Stir thoroughly and drop a slice of orange into the drink. Serve with a stirrer.

Harvey Wallbanger

1 ms vodka
4 ms orange juice
½ ms Galliano

Fill a tall glass with ice, then add the vodka and orange juice. Stir thoroughly, then splash Galliano on top.

Egghead

1 ms vodka
4 ms orange juice
1 egg

Blend all the ingredients together on fast speed for 5 seconds, then pour into a tall glass filled with ice. Decorate with a slice of orange and a red cocktail cherry. Serve with straws.

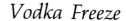

Vodka Freeze

(Illustrated on page 34)

2 ms vodka
1 ms Bols Dry Orange Curacao
2 scoops orange sorbet

Blend the vodka, orange curacao and one scoop of orange sorbet together on slow speed for 5 seconds, then pour into a sundae glass and drop in the second scoop of orange sorbet. Decorate with a slice of orange and serve with straws.

Swizzles

The Swizzle originated in the British West Indies, the land of sugar and dark rum. It must be drunk as cold as possible, therefore the drink was traditionally served with a small stick which was swizzled furiously back and forth between the palms of the hands until the glass frosted over. The blender banishes all this hard work and produces a refreshing iced drink in a few seconds.

The Swizzle

2 ms dark rum
1 ms fresh lime juice
½ ms sugar syrup
2 dashes Angostura bitters

Fill a tall glass with crushed ice and pour in the ingredients. Stir until the glass is frosted. Decorate with a sprig of mint and serve with a swizzle stick.

Frozen Swizzle

2 ms dark rum
1 ms fresh lime juice
½ ms sugar syrup
2 dashes Angostura bitters
1 scoop crushed ice

Blend all the ingredients together on slow speed for 5 seconds, then pour into a tall glass filled with ice. Decorate with a sprig of mint and serve with a swizzle stick.

Gin Swizzle

Same as The Swizzle, except gin is used instead of rum.

Mai Tai

1 ms light rum
1 ms golden rum
½ ms Bols Dry Orange Curacao
½ ms fresh lime juice
2 dashes orgeat syrup
1 dash grenadine
1 scoop crushed ice

Blend all the ingredients together on slow speed for 5 seconds, then pour into an old-fashioned glass filled with ice. Decorate with a slice of lime, a red cocktail cherry and a sprig of mint and serve with a swizzle stick.

Scorpion

2 ms golden rum
1 ms orange juice
1 ms fresh lemon juice
½ ms brandy
2 dashes orgeat syrup
1 scoop crushed ice

Blend all the ingredients together on slow speed for 5 seconds, then pour into a medium-size glass. Decorate with a slice of orange and a sprig of mint. Serve with a swizzle stick.

Zombie

1 ms light rum
1 ms golden rum
1 ms dark rum
1 ms fresh lime juice
1 ms pineapple juice
½ ms Bols Apricot Brandy
½ ms 151-proof Demeraran rum
1 teaspoon fine sugar
2 scoops crushed ice

Blend together all except the 151-proof rum on slow speed for 5 seconds, then pour into a very large bowl-type glass filled with ice. Drop in slices of lime and orange. Decorate with a wedge of pineapple and a sprig of mint. Finally splash in the 151-proof rum just before drinking and serve with a swizzle stick.

GIN: *spirit of the British Empire*

The Englishman has always been fond of his tipple and through the centuries has popularized many beverages – most of the best cognac has always been shipped to England, port was drunk exclusively by the English in the early days, sherry and champagne were first exported to England and the Royal Navy spread the fame of rum. However, it was gin that the English adopted as their own spirit, although they did not invent it.

Mr. Lucas Bols is known to have been distilling a type of gin on the outskirts of Amsterdam in the late 1500s. The early gins were made by taking the raw spirit that had been distilled from rye and re-distilling it with juniper berries to flavour the spirit. These berries have been used since ancient times as a diuretic and physicians prescribed their use for treatment of kidney complaints, so it is highly likely that the first gins were of a medicinal nature. The Dutch referred to the drink as *genièvre*, the French word for juniper. When Queen Elizabeth I sent troops to Holland to fight with the Dutch Protestants against the Spanish and French Catholics, the soldiers discovered the spirit in plentiful supply. They drank it to keep warm and to stave off hunger, and found it so fortified them before battle that they spoke of it as 'Dutch Courage'. The English soldiers found *genièvre* difficult to say, so they corrupted it to 'gin', which it has been ever since, although the gentry used the more polite term of 'Hollands' to describe the spirit.

The English began distilling gin themselves and, being cheap to produce, it was within reach of the working class. These people were extremely poor and used gin to relieve their worries, giving rise to the bad reputation the spirit had in the 17th–18th centuries. However, by the 19th century, gin had achieved respectability. Victorian ladies would partake of it 'for their health', the public houses were glass and gas lamp palaces devoted to the sale of gin and it was to be found in liquor cabinets of the gentry – although the decanter often had a neck label saying 'white wine' as it was thought inadvisable to let the servants know the contents.

In Victorian days, if the Navy was said to have sailed on rum, then the Army marched on gin, as a goodly supply of it went with them. The English tea planters in India and the rubber planters in Malaya would enjoy their late afternoon gins under the shade of the verandah, the British traders in Singapore were fond of their gin slings and the officers on Her Majesty's ships would sip gently at their pink gins as they guarded the far-flung Empire. The invention of tonic helped to cement the link between gin and the English in the tropics as quinine, the flavouring used in tonic, is a known antidote for malaria.

Gin produced in London has been so widely distributed in the last century that it is now regarded as a style, and brands such as Beefeater, Gilbeys and Gordons are known as London Dry gins. They are produced by distilling neutral spirit with a variety of berries and spices which impart the characteristic aroma that makes gin such an instantly recognizable spirit. Gin produced in Holland has such a distinctive flavour of its own that it is rarely used in cocktails. *Genever*, the Dutch word for gin, is produced by distilling berries and spices with a spirit made from malted grain, so the drink is sometimes nicknamed Dutch whisky. The style known as Old Genever was Holland's national drink until about forty years ago when demand for the lighter Young Genever began increasing as its less pronounced flavour mixes well with minerals and fruit juices.

LONDON
1873·1911·1924

Party Time

Party drinks need to be made with a minimum of fuss and last minute preparation. The blender is an invaluable piece of equipment at a party as it can mix drinks in multiples in just a few moments, so not only the first tray of drinks looks exciting but the refills are also fresh and appetizing. Most of the recipes in this book can be made for more than one person by simply multiplying the stated measures by the number of drinks required. However, the recipes in this chapter are specifically designed for parties, so the number of drinks made by any one recipe is mentioned as well.

When deciding which drinks to serve to guests be careful not to be too ambitious. A recipe with eight ingredients is easy to mix for a few people but is impractical for large gatherings because of time involved in preparation as well as the considerable expense. Also, drinks requiring intricate decoration are not especially suitable for parties because of the time factor. It is wise to be conservative with the amount of alcohol in the drinks. If you offer highly alcoholic drinks to thirsty new arrivals they are likely to show the effects very quickly.

The Blender

Set the machine up in the kitchen in its own special area, preferably not too far from the sink. Have the necessary stock of bottles within easy reach and check that glass cloths and sponges are nearby, so that any cleaning can be done quickly. It is of great assistance to have two blenders when entertaining, as this makes preparation much faster and allows a choice of drinks to be offered around at the same time. In this case, one blender can be reserved for any recipes containing cream, coconut cream or ice cream as these substances tend to coat the inside of the jug.

Glassware

It is better to have too many glasses than not enough, not only because washing up should be kept to manageable proportions, but because a shortage of glasses can mean a shortage of drinks which hints at lack of planning. Glassware can be hired quite easily from many outlets that sell liquor and the most useful styles for large gatherings are the all-purpose goblet and the tall highball glass, both of which are sturdy and easily cleaned. Parties are not the time for prized crystal glasses or intricately designed styles which take time to clean properly. Also, trays are of immense assistance because they reduce the amount of legwork.

Ice and Garnish

Bags of ice are readily available and it is wise to refreeze them thoroughly after purchase as melting ice is of no advantage at all. Large cubes are more efficient at chilling a drink than small ones which melt too quickly, and although well packed crushed ice will keep a drink quite cold, it takes considerable time to fill and re-fill a large number of glasses with it. Choose drinks with simple decoration that can be easily prepared in advance and will not wilt when it is left covered with plastic in the refrigerator. Citrus fruit can be sliced and nicked so that it can be quickly slipped over the rims of glasses when required and cherries are no trouble to drop into the drinks if they have been well drained beforehand, while coloured straws add a touch of brightness as well as help guests to recognize their own drinks.

Right: Strawberry Blonde

Over Ice

The following drinks can easily be made in quantity by mixing a whole blender jug full of the mixture and pouring into ice-filled glasses. There are no carbonated minerals included in these recipes, so they can be made in advance and refrigerated then given a final whizz to freshen them up before serving to the guests.

Bloody Mary

(Illustrated on front cover and page 15)

6 drinks

10 oz/300 ml (U.S. 1¼ cups) vodka
24 oz/700 ml (U.S. 3 cups) tomato juice
2 oz/60 ml (U.S. ¼ cup) fresh lemon juice
1 oz/30 ml (U.S. 2 tablespoons) Worcestershire sauce
2 teaspoons celery salt

Blend all the ingredients together on fast speed for 10 seconds, then pour into tall glasses filled with ice. Decorate with sticks of celery which can also be used to stir the drinks.

The addition of horseradish sauce makes an interesting variation to the drink.

Florida Comfort

6 drinks

100 oz/300 ml (U.S. 1¼ cups) Southern Comfort
5 oz/150 ml (U.S. ⅔ cup) fresh lemon juice
20 oz/600 ml (U.S. 2½ cups) orange juice
1 oz/30 ml (U.S. 2 tablespoons) grenadine

Blend all the ingredients together on fast speed for 10 seconds, then pour into tall glasses filled with ice and drop in slices of orange. Serve with stirrers.

Knuckleduster

(Illustrated on page 49)

6 drinks

6 oz/175 ml (U.S. ¾ cup) Malibu coconut liqueur
6 oz/175 ml (U.S. ¾ cup) Bols Blue Curacao
20 oz/600 ml (U.S. 2½ cups) pineapple juice

Blend all the ingredients together on fast speed for 5 seconds, then pour into tall glasses filled with ice.

Pink Grapefruit

(Illustrated on page 49)

10 drinks

8 oz/225 ml (U.S. 1 cup) Malibu coconut liqueur
16 oz/450 ml (U.S. 2 cups) grapefruit juice
2 oz/60 ml (U.S. ¼ cup) Campari

Blend the Malibu and grapefruit juice together on fast speed for 5 seconds, then pour into medium-size glasses filled with crushed ice. Splash the Campari on the top.

Rusty River

6 glasses

9 oz/250 ml (U.S. 1 cup) Southern Comfort
15 oz/425 ml (U.S. scant 2 cups) grapefruit juice
3 oz/90 ml (U.S. 5 tablespoons) Bols brown Crème de Cacao

Blend all the ingredients together on fast speed for 7 seconds, then pour into tall glasses filled with ice.

Snow Float

12 glasses

10 oz / 300 ml (U.S. 1¼ cups) Bols
Chocolate Mint
10 oz / 300 ml (U.S. 1¼ cups) milk
6 scoops vanilla ice cream

Blend all the ingredients together on slow speed for 5 seconds, then pour into small glasses. Sprinkle coconut on top.

Top-Ups

Recipes that require topping up with a carbonated mineral just prior to serving are excellent drinks for making in multiples, as a batch of the base mixture can be prepared in the blender. It is simply a matter of topping up with the appropriate mineral to yield an array of appetizing cocktails.

Cool Caribbean

12 drinks

10 oz / 300 ml (U.S. 1¼ cups) Malibu
Coconut Liqueur
5 oz / 150 ml (U.S. ⅔ cup) Bols Crème de
Banane
15 oz / 450 ml (U.S. scant 2 cups) orange
juice
soda water

Blend together all except the soda water on fast speed for 5 seconds, then divide equally amongst tall glasses filled with ice. Top up the drinks with soda water and decorate with a red cocktail cherry. Serve with stirrers and straws.

Highland Tea

8 drinks

4 oz / 120 ml (U.S. ½ cup) Drambuie
8 oz / 225 ml (U.S. 1 cup) vodka
5 oz / 150 ml (U.S. ⅔ cup) cold weak tea
Coca-Cola

Blend together all except the Coca-Cola on fast speed for 5 seconds, then divide equally amongst tall glasses filled with ice. Top up the drinks with Coca-Cola. Serve with stirrers and straws.

Katzweasel

10 drinks

8 oz / 225 ml (U.S. 1 cup) gin
12 oz / 350 ml (U.S. 1½ cups) orange juice
4 oz / 120 ml (U.S. ½ cup) lemon juice
2 oz / 60 ml (U.S. ¼ cup) sugar syrup
1 egg white
tonic water

Blend together all except the tonic water on slow speed for 5 seconds, then divide equally amongst tall glasses filled with ice. Top up the drinks with tonic water and drop in slices of lemon. Serve with stirrers and straws.

Paddlesteamer

12 drinks

7 oz / 200 ml (U.S. ¾ cup) Southern
Comfort
8 oz / 225 ml (U.S. 1 cup) vodka
15 oz / 425 ml (U.S. scant 2 cups) orange
juice
ginger ale

Blend together all except the ginger ale on fast speed for 5 seconds, then divide equally amongst tall glasses filled with ice. Top up the drinks with ginger ale and drop in slices of orange. Serve with stirrers and straws.

Pineapple Freeze

(Illustrated below)

15 drinks

10 oz / 300 ml (U.S. 1¼ cups) golden rum
20 oz / 600 ml (U.S. 2½ cups) pineapple
juice
2 oz / 60 ml (U.S. ¼ cup) sugar syrup
1 egg white
lemonade

Blend together all except the lemonade on
slow speed for 5 seconds, then divide
equally amongst tall glasses or pineapple
shells filled with ice. Top up the drinks
with lemonade and decorate with a wedge
of pineapple and a red cocktail cherry, or
serve with straws if using pineapple shells.

Planters Punch

8 drinks

10 oz / 300 ml (U.S. 1¼ cups) dark rum
15 oz / 450 ml (U.S. scant 2 cups) lemon
juice
5 oz / 150 ml (U.S. ⅔ cup) orange juice
2 oz / 60 ml (U.S. ¼ cup) grenadine
8 dashes Angostura bitters
soda water

Blend together all except the soda water
on fast speed for 5 seconds, then divide
equally amongst tall glasses filled with ice.
Top up the drinks with soda water and
drop in slices of orange and lemon. Serve
with stirrers and straws.

Strawberry Blonde

(Illustrated on page 45)

24 drinks

6 oz/175 ml (U.S. ¾ cup) Irish Mist
1 lb/450 g strawberries
4 bottles dry sparkling white wine

Put the Irish Mist and half the strawberries into the blender jug and blend on slow speed until puréed. Add the remaining strawberries to the mixture and blend on low speed until smooth. Divide equally amongst champagne glasses and top up with chilled sparkling white wine. Decorate with a strawberry.

Left to right: *Pineapple Freeze, Waterloo, Juicy Lucy, Cuba Libre, Pink Grapefruit, Knuckleduster*

Punches

A punch lends a special touch to a party as it shows the host or hostess has gone to some trouble to make the guests feel welcome. Most punches can be made well in advance of the event and extra supplies can be kept in the kitchen, ready to replenish the punch bowl. This section includes some that make use of the blender and a hot cup that would bring a warm glow to Aunt Mary's cheeks on a cold winter's morning.

Bride's Bowl

30 4-oz/120-ml drinks

2 8-oz/225-g cans pineapple chunks
8 oz/225 ml (U.S. 1 cup) pineapple juice
8 oz/225 ml (U.S. 1 cup) fresh lemon
juice
2 oz/60 ml (U.S. ¼ cup) sugar syrup
1 bottle light rum
2 large bottles soda water
2 lb/900 g strawberries

Blend together the canned pineapple (with its syrup), the pineapple juice, lemon juice and sugar syrup with half the rum on slow speed for 15 seconds. Chill for 24 hours. Pour into a punch bowl filled with ice and add the remainder of the rum and the soda water. Slice the strawberries and drop them into the punch. Stir gently.

Eggnog

10 5-oz/150-ml drinks

6 egg yolks
6 egg whites
6 oz/175 g (U.S. ¾ cup) sugar
8 oz/225 ml (U.S. 1 cup) milk
8 oz/225 ml (U.S. 1 cup) cream
16 oz/450 ml (U.S. 2 cups) whipped
cream
8 oz/225 ml (U.S. 1 cup) dark rum
4 oz/120 ml (U.S. ½ cup) brandy
4 oz/120 ml (U.S. ½ cup) Bols Apricot
Brandy

Beat the egg whites until stiff. Blend the egg yolks and sugar on medium speed until light and creamy. Pour in the milk, blending all the time. Then add the cream, rum, brandy and apricot brandy and blend on slow speed for 3 seconds. Fold the egg whites into the whipped cream, then gently stir this into the mixture in a large bowl. Refrigerate until chilled and dust with nutmeg.

Party Punch

28 5-oz/150-ml drinks

8 oz/225 ml (U.S. 1 cup) pineapple juice
8 oz/225 ml (U.S. 1 cup) grapefruit juice
4 oz/120 ml (U.S. ½ cup) fresh lemon juice
1 bottle Southern Comfort
4 oz/120 ml (U.S. ½ cup) Bols Peach
Brandy
2 large bottles lemonade

Pre-chill ingredients. Mix together all except the lemonade in a large ice-filled bowl, then add the lemonade before serving. Garnish with slices of fruit in season.

Pennsylvania

20 5-oz/150-ml drinks

10 oz/300 ml (U.S. 1¼ cups) Jack Daniels
10 oz/300 ml (U.S. 1¼ cups) Bols Peach
Brandy
10 oz/300 ml (U.S. 1¼ cups) brandy
10 oz/300 ml (U.S. 1¼ cups) Southern
Comfort
1 small can peaches
1 small can apricots
1 bottle red wine
1 large bottle ginger ale

Blend together half the Jack Daniels, peach brandy, brandy and Southern Comfort with the canned peaches on low speed for 10 seconds and pour into a large bowl. Then blend the rest of the spirit with the canned apricots on slow speed for 10 seconds and add to the bowl. Pour in the bottle of red wine and stir gently. Add slices of fruit and chill for 24 hours. Add ice and the ginger ale before serving.

Riding House Stirrup Cup

25 3-oz/90-ml drinks

1 bottle red wine
1 bottle cider
7 oz/200 ml (U.S. ¾ cup) dark rum
3 dashes Angostura bitters
1 teaspoon cinnamon
3 cloves
8 oz/225 ml (U.S. 1 cup) orange juice
4 oz/120 ml (U.S. ½ cup) sugar

Gently heat all the ingredients except the cider in a saucepan until thoroughly warm, but do not allow the mixture to boil. Add the cider and serve in small cups.

Sangria

8 5-oz/150-ml drinks

1 bottle red wine
2 oz/55 g sugar
8 oz/225 ml water
1 thinly sliced orange
1 thinly sliced lime
1 thinly sliced lemon
8 oz/225 ml soda water

Dissolve the sugar in the water in a large jug. Add the fruit and wine and refrigerate for an hour. Before serving, add the soda water and some ice cubes.

Strawberry Bowl

20 5-oz/150-ml drinks

3 bottles chilled moselle wine
1 bottle chilled champagne
2 lb/1 kg sliced strawberries
8 tablespoons (U.S. ⅔ cup) sugar

Sprinkle the strawberries with sugar, pour one bottle of moselle over them and refrigerate for several hours. Before serving, pour into a large bowl with ice and add the remaining bottles of moselle and champagne. Serve in small wine glasses.

Trixie Punch

12 5-oz/150-ml drinks

7 oz/200 ml gin
15 oz/425 ml Southern Comfort
7 oz/200 ml lime juice
8 slices pineapple
2 oz/30 ml grenadine
20 oz/600 ml creaming soda

Blend together all except the creaming soda on slow speed for 20 seconds, then pour into a large bowl filled with ice. Decorate with slices of orange, add the creaming soda and serve immediately.

Unblended favourites

These drinks are all made straight into the glass, so they can be quickly prepared in multiples by lining up as many glasses as are required and mixing the drinks all at once. They are simple flavoursome combinations meant to be made just prior to being served, so prepare any necessary decoration in advance. The empty glasses should be on a tray ready to be offered around while the drinks retain their freshness and sparkle.

Blue Lagoon

1 ms vodka
1 ms Bols Blue Curacao
lemonade

Pour the vodka and blue curacao into a tall glass filled with ice and top up with lemonade.

Cactus Café

1 ms Bols Coffee Liqueur
½ ms tequila
lemonade

Pour the coffee liqueur and tequila into a tall glass filled with ice and top up with lemonade.

Cuba Libre

(Illustrated on page 49)

2 ms light rum
1 ms fresh lime juice
Coca-Cola

Pour the rum and lime juice into a tall glass filled with ice and top up with Coca-Cola. Drop in a slice of lime and serve with a stirrer.

Gin Sling

2 ms gin
1 ms lemon juice
3 ms soda water

Pour the gin and lemon juice into a tall glass filled with ice and top up with soda water.

Icebreaker

2 ms Pernod
3 ms bitter lemon

Pour the ingredients into a tall glass filled with ice and serve with a stirrer.

Juicy Lucy

(Illustrated on page 49)

2 ms Galliano
4 ms orange juice

Pour the ingredients into a tall glass or goblet filled with ice and serve with a stirrer.

Kir

1 teaspoon crème de cassis
5 oz / 150 ml (U.S. ⅔ cup) dry white wine

Pour the cassis into a white wine glass and top with the white wine.

Little Sister

1 ms gin
1 ms Bols Dry Orange Curacao
orange juice

Pour the gin and curacao into a tall glass filled with ice and top up with orange juice.

Machete

1 ms vodka
2 ms pineapple juice
3 ms tonic

Mix all the ingredients together in a tall glass filled with ice.

Moscow Mule

2 ms vodka
4 ms ginger beer
½ ms lime cordial

Pour the ingredients into a tall glass filled with ice and drop in a slice of lime.

Pigs in Space

1 ms golden rum
2 dashes Angostura bitters
dry ginger ale

Stir the rum and Angostura bitters together in a tall glass filled with ice and top up with ginger ale. Add a twist of orange peel.

Pimms

(Illustrated on page 15)

1½ ms Pimms
lemonade

Pour Pimms into a tall glass filled with ice and top up with lemonade. Decorate with a sliver of cucumber skin and a slice of lemon. Serve with straws.

Rembrandt

1 teaspoon Bols Apricot Brandy
5 oz/150 ml (U.S. ⅔ cup) dry white wine

Pour the apricot brandy into a wine glass and top with the white wine.

Shark Strangler

1 ms Malibu
1 dash lime cordial
Coca-Cola

Pour the Malibu and lime cordial into a tall glass filled with ice and top up with Coca-Cola. Drop in a slice of lime and serve with a stirrer.

Snapdragon

2 ms vodka
1 ms Bols Crème de Menthe
soda water

Pour the vodka and crème de menthe into
a tall glass filled with ice and top up with
soda water.

Stone Fence

1 ms whisky
2 dashes Angostura bitters
cider

Pour the whisky and bitters into a tall glass
filled with ice and top up with cider.

Tiger's Tail

2 ms Pernod
3 ms orange juice

Pour the ingredients into a tall glass filled
with ice and serve with a stirrer.

Vermouth Cassis

1 teaspoon crème de cassis
5 oz/150 ml (U.S. ⅔ cup) dry vermouth

Pour the cassis into a wine glass and top
with the dry vermouth.

Waterloo

(Illustrated on page 49)

1 ms Mandarine Napoleon
4 ms bitter lemon

Pour the ingredients into a tall glass filled
with ice and drop in a slice of lemon. Serve
with a stirrer.

White Lightning

1 ms vodka
1 ms Bols Kummel
tonic

Pour the vodka and kummel into a tall
glass filled with ice and top up with tonic.

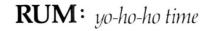

RUM: *yo-ho-ho time*

No sailor worth his salt nor pirate worth his Jolly Roger would be without his ration of rum to fortify him against the rigors of his greatest adversary, the sea. Rum and the sea have long been associated together, so it is fitting that the sea should have played a major role in the rise of the spirit to international significance.

Rum is derived from sugar cane, a plant known to have been growing in India as early as 327 B.C. In medieval times the Arab traders brought sugar overland to Europe, where it was regarded as a highly prized luxury, although some of the plant was able to be cultivated in the Canary Islands. It was from here that Columbus obtained the cane cuttings he carried with him on his epic sea voyage to the Americas and those cuttings were the beginnings of what is now the major economic crop of the West Indies. The Spanish, who had financed Columbus's expedition, began settling in the Caribbean. They took with them the knowledge of distillation, so by A.D. 1600 the fiery alcoholic beverage distilled from fermented sugar was freely available on most of the islands. It was aptly named Rumbullion, a word meaning 'rumpus', because of the uproar caused by those who had been drinking it. The natives also called it Kill Devil, which may be a reference to their use of the spirit as an antiseptic and general medicine.

Enterprising sea captains who carried slaves to the West Indies began shipping 'rum' to Europe on the return voyage and sailors took it to warm themselves on the long voyage and as a means of staving off hunger pains. The spirit found such favour with the English sailors that in the mid 17th century the Royal Navy began issuing a daily half pint of rum to every sailor, a tradition that continued for over three hundred years until it ceased in 1970. In the navy it was used freely as a preventive against scurvy, a cure for colds, an anaesthetic before operations and as fortification against the weather. It was nicknamed 'Nelson's Blood' after the Battle of Trafalgar, as the revered man's body was preserved in a cask of rum to be shipped back to England, although it is rumoured that the cask was empty of spirit when it arrived on shore, the contents having been drunk by the crew.

Rum has also contributed to the richness of colloquial English. The order to 'splice the mainbrace' on board ship was the signal to issue an extra tot of rum, and once the sun was 'over the yardarm' of the ship it was time to partake of the daily ration. Also, the expression 'groggy', to describe someone unsteady on his legs, is derived from the British Navy's association with rum. A certain Admiral Vernon, known as Old Grog because of his famous grogram coat, whilst on duty in the Spanish Main ordered that the rum ration of his sailors be watered down to reduce the amount of drunkenness on board. His crew called the watered rum 'grog' to show their displeasure at this action, so that those who had too much grog became groggy. A strange way for a British Admiral to enter the ranks of the immortals.

Creamy Concoctions

After Eight

1 ms whisky
1 ms Royal Mint Chocolate Liqueur
1 ms cream

Blend all the ingredients together on slow speed for 15 seconds. Pour into a cocktail glass and grate chocolate on top.

Australian Dream

1 ms Bols Crème de Banane
1 ms strawberry liqueur
1 ms orange juice
1 scoop ice cream

Blend all the ingredients together on slow speed for 10 seconds. Pour into a medium-size glass and garnish with a diced strawberry.

Banshee

1 ms Bols white Crème de Cacao
1 ms Bols Crème de Banane
1 ms cream
1 scoop crushed ice

Blend all the ingredients together on medium speed for 10 seconds then pour into a medium-size glass.

Easter Egg

(Illustrated on front cover)

1 ms Bols Chocolate Mint
1 ms Bols Advocaat
1 scoop vanilla ice cream

Blend all the ingredients together on slow speed for 10 seconds, then pour into a medium-size glass.

Fairy Queen

1 ms vodka
½ ms Bols Coffee Liqueur
½ ms Galliano
½ ms cream
2 ice cubes

Blend all the ingredients together on fast speed for 5 seconds then pour into a cocktail glass.

Frozen Mandarin Sour

2 ms Mandarine Napoleon
1 ms fresh lemon juice
1 scoop vanilla ice cream

Blend all the ingredients together on slow speed for 7 seconds then pour into a medium-size goblet.

56

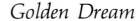

Frozen Melon Sour

2 ms Midori melon liqueur
1 ms fresh lemon juice
1 scoop vanilla ice cream

Blend all the ingredients together on slow speed for 7 seconds then pour into a medium-size glass.

Frozen Steppes

2 ms vodka
1 ms Bols brown Crème de Cacao
1 scoop vanilla ice cream

Blend all the ingredients together on slow speed for 7 seconds, then pour into a medium-size glass.

Glacier

2 ms brandy
1 ms cream
1 ms orange juice
2 dashes sugar syrup
2 ice cubes

Blend all the ingredients together on slow speed for 10 seconds, then pour into a medium-size glass.

Glass Slipper

1 ms Bols Kummel
1 ms vodka
1 scoop vanilla ice cream

Blend all the ingredients together on slow speed for 10 seconds then pour into a medium-size glass.

Golden Dream

½ ms Galliano
½ ms brandy
½ ms orange juice
1 dash egg white

Blend all the ingredients together on slow speed for 7 seconds, then pour into a cocktail glass. Place a twist of orange on top.

Gretna Green

1 ms light rum
½ ms Bols green Crème de Menthe
½ ms coconut cream
1 ms pineapple juice
1 scoop crushed ice

Blend all the ingredients together on slow speed for 10 seconds, then pour into a medium-size glass.

Guinness Cooler

(Illustrated on page 57)

½ ms Bols Coffee Liqueur
½ ms Cointreau
1 ms Dubonnet
½ bottle Guinness

Blend together all except the Guinness on fast speed for 5 seconds, then pour into a tall glass filled with ice. Top up with Guinness and drop in a spiral of apple skin.

Humming Bird

1 ms gin
1 ms passionfruit nectar
½ ms Bols Blue Curacao
1 large slice melon
1 scoop crushed ice

Blend all the ingredients together on slow speed for 10 seconds, then pour into a large bowl-type glass.

Mexican Dream

1 ms Malibu Coconut Liqueur
1 ms gold tequila
1 scoop strawberry ice cream
1 dash strawberry liqueur

Blend all the ingredients together on slow speed for 10 seconds, then pour into a medium-size glass.

Midnight Cowboy

1 ms gin
½ ms Bols Coffee Liqueur
½ ms cream
Coca-Cola

Blend together all except the Coca-Cola on fast speed for 5 seconds, then pour into a tall glass filled with ice. Top up with Coca-Cola and serve with a stirrer and straws.

Midnight Lace

1 ms light rum
½ ms Bols Chocolate Mint
1 scoop vanilla ice cream

Blend all the ingredients together on slow speed for 10 seconds, then pour into a medium-size glass. Sprinkle cinnamon on top.

Mississippi Mud

1 ms Southern Comfort
½ ms Bols Coffee Liqueur
1 scoop vanilla ice cream

Blend all the ingredients together on slow speed for 10 seconds, then pour into a medium-size glass.

Peachie

2 ms Bols Peach Brandy
1 half peach
1 scoop vanilla ice cream

Blend all the ingredients together on slow speed for 10 seconds, then pour into a medium-size glass. Decorate with a slice of peach.

Petit Four

1 ms Bols brown Crème de Cacao
½ ms Bols Crème de Banane
1 ms peach nectar
1 scoop chocolate ice cream

Blend all the ingredients together on slow speed for 10 seconds, then pour into a medium-size glass. Serve with a chocolate flake.

Grasshopper

(Illustrated on page 65)

1 ms Bols green Crème de Menthe
1 ms Bols white Crème de Cacao
1 ms cream
2 ice cubes

Blend all the ingredients together on slow speed for 10 seconds, then pour into a cocktail glass.

Rum 'n' Raisin

(Illustrated left)

1 ms dark rum
½ ms Bols Chocolate Mint
1 scoop chocolate ice cream
1 tablespoon seedless raisins

Blend all the ingredients together on slow speed for 15 seconds, then pour into a cocktail glass. Serve with short straws.

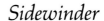

Raffles

1 ms Dubonnet
½ ms Bols Coffee Liqueur
½ ms calvados
Guinness
2 ice cubes

Blend together all except the Guinness on fast speed for 7 seconds, then pour into a large glass filled with ice. Top up with Guinness. Decorate with a slice of orange.

Sambuca Whirl

1ms sambuca
1ms light rum
1ms lime juice
1ms cream
1 scoop crushed ice

Blend all the ingredients together on slow speed for 10 seconds, then pour into a tulip glass. Serve with straws.

Saronnada

1 ms vodka
½ ms Amaretto di Saronno
¼ ms coconut cream
1 ms pineapple juice
2 ice cubes

Blend all the ingredients together on medium speed for 10 seconds, then pour into a tall glass filled with ice. Decorate with a wedge of pineapple and a red cocktail cherry. Serve with straws.

White Russian

1 ms vodka
½ ms Kahlua
1 ms cream
2 ice cubes

Blend all the ingredients together on slow speed for 10 seconds, then pour into a medium-size glass filled with ice.

Sidewinder

1 ms vodka
½ ms Amaretto
¼ ms Bols white Crème de Cacao
¼ ms white crème de menthe
1 scoop vanilla ice cream

Blend all the ingredients together on slow speed for 10 seconds, then pour into a medium-size glass.

Silk Stockings

1 ms tequila
½ ms Bols white Crème de Cacao
1 ms cream
dash grenadine
1 scoop crushed ice

Blend all the ingredients together on slow speed for 10 seconds, then pour into a tulip glass and sprinkle cinnamon on top. Serve with straws.

Sunny Dream

1 ms Bols Apricot Brandy
½ ms Cointreau
3 ms orange juice
1 scoop vanilla ice cream

Blend all the ingredients together on slow speed for 10 seconds, then pour into a medium-size glass. Decorate with a slice of orange.

Velvet Hammer

1 ms Bols Dry Orange Curacao
1 ms Tia Maria
1 ms cream
2 ice cubes

Blend all the ingredients together on slow speed for 10 seconds, then pour into a cocktail glass.

Strawberries and Cream

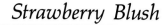

Flamingo Pink

(Illustrated on page 65)

1 ms light rum
1 ms grapefruit juice
1 ms cream
6 strawberries
2 ice cubes

Blend all the ingredients together on slow speed for 15 seconds, then pour into a small cocktail glass and decorate with a strawberry.

Pink Squirrel

1 ms light rum
½ ms strawberry liqueur
1 scoop strawberry ice cream

Blend all the ingredients together on slow speed for 10 seconds, then pour into a cocktail glass. Decorate with a strawberry.

Strawberry Fair

1 ms tequila
3 strawberries
1 tablespoon cranberry juice
cream
2 dashes black pepper

Blend all the ingredients together on slow speed for 10 seconds, then pour into a medium-size glass filled with crushed ice and decorate with two red cocktail cherries. Serve with short straws.

Strawberry Blush

2 ms vodka
1 scoop vanilla ice cream
½ ms strawberry syrup
3 strawberries

Blend all the ingredients together on slow speed for 10 seconds, then pour into a medium-size glass. Decorate with a strawberry and serve with straws.

Teardrop

1 ms gin
2 ms orange juice
1 ms cream
½ ms strawberry syrup

Blend together all except the strawberry syrup on fast speed for 5 seconds, then pour into a long glass filled with crushed ice. Splash strawberry syrup on top and serve with straws.

Teddy Bear

2 ms light rum
2 ms Bols Advocaat
3 strawberries
lemonade

Blend together all except the lemonade on slow speed for 10 seconds, then pour into a medium-size glass filled with ice. Top with lemonade. Decorate with a strawberry and serve with straws.

Strawberry Dawn

(Illustrated right)

2 ms gin
1 ms coconut cream
3 strawberries
1 scoop crushed ice

Blend all the ingredients together on slow speed until smooth, then pour into a medium-size glass and decorate with a strawberry. Serve with straws.

Ramos Fizz

(Illustrated right)

2 ms gin
1 ms fresh lemon juice
1 ms cream
2 dashes sugar syrup
1 dash orange flower water
2 ice cubes

Blend all the ingredients together on slow speed for 15 seconds, then pour into a small highball glass.

Strawberry Kiss

(Illustrated below)

1 ms Jack Daniels
1 ms strawberry syrup
3 strawberries
2 ice cubes
cream

Blend together all except the cream on slow speed for 10 seconds, then pour into a small flute glass and float cream on top.

Left to right: *Flamingo Pink, Grasshopper, Strawberry Dawn, Ramos Fizz, Strawberry Kiss*

Liqueurs Colours on parade

Modern liqueurs come in a full array of colours that make them excellent ingredients and fun to use when making cocktails. However, the first liqueurs were medicinal potions mixed by physicians and monks who understood the healing properties of plants. For example, there are records of ancient Greek physicians prescribing caraway-flavoured liquor to settle upset stomachs, while the monks of the Bénédictine monastery at Fécamp in France administered their herbal potion as a defence against malaria. The method used to make the early liqueurs was quite simple. The bark, seeds, flowers and leaves of certain herbs and other plants were steeped in alcohol to extract their essential oils, so the alcohol took on the same properties as the herbs and plants. Often the mixture was quite bitter, so sugar was added to sweeten it and make it palatable for the patient.

The Italians were the first to drink the potions for pleasure rather than as a cure, and when Catherine de'Medici went to France in 1533 as bride of the heir to the French throne, she made fashionable there the idea of liqueurs as after dinner drinks. As a result of this, Bénédictine became a favourite at the Royal Court and enterprising souls began producing liqueurs on a commercial scale to satisfy the increasing demand. One such gentleman was Lucas Bols who, in 1575, founded one of the oldest distilling firms still in existence. Amsterdam was well sited for such a business as Holland had a flourishing trade with the New World which supplied the raw materials such as coffee, cocoa, sugar and exotic spices necessary to make the liqueurs.

The fruit liqueurs originated from the need to preserve the abundant summer fruits for use through the long winters. Apricots, peaches, cherries and other fruits were pricked all over, then steeped in alcohol for a few months. During this time, the liquor took on the colour and flavour of the fruit, so it only required straining and sweetening to produce a delicious liqueur. Until the turn of this century, many European housewives were very proud of their own home-made fruit liqueurs and no recipe book was complete without a few hints on how to prepare them.

There are literally thousands of liqueurs throughout the world, some recognized internationally and others known only within the local area of production. Some of the most famous are mentioned here.

Herb-based liqueurs

Bénédictine A very sweet amber coloured liqueur with a strong herby aroma. It is one of the oldest liqueurs in the world and is still produced in France, where it was first made by monks of the Bénédictine monastery at Fécamp in Normandy. The same firm now markets B & B, which is a blend of Bénédictine and brandy, so it is lighter and drier than the neat liqueur.

Brontë A spicy sweet blend of honey and herbs sold in a squat pottery jug. It is produced in Yorkshire, which was also the home of the famous Brontë sisters.

Centerbe This highly alcoholic Italian liqueur is said to be compounded from 100 herbs, hence its name, although it has a pronounced mint flavour.

Chartreuse The monks of La Grande Chartreuse monastry near Grenoble in France have been producing this liqueur for over 300 years. It is made from over 130 herbs and spices and is available in two different alcoholic strengths. The potent green Chartreuse has an assertive herby taste, while the yellow Chartreuse is sweeter, softer and less alcoholic.

Cordial Médoc This red brown liqueur comes from the Bordeaux region of France, so it is appropriate that it has a predominantly claret base which is flavoured with herbs and fruits.

Drambuie A Scottish liqueur based on fine old Scotch malt whisky flavoured with herbs and honey. The name is derived from the Gaelic *an dram buidheach* which translates as 'the drink that satisfies'.

Galliano A golden yellow herb liqueur from Italy. It has a lemon-aniseed flavour and is sold in distinctive tall flute bottles. It is named in honour of Major Galliano, an Italian soldier whose unit held off a force eighty times its own number for forty-four days during the Abyssinian campaign in 1895.

Gold Liqueur Gold has always been credited with curative powers and a goldwasser was made in the Free City of Danzig almost 400 years ago. The modern Gold Liqueur is a clear liquid flavoured with caraway, aniseed and other herbs bound together with curacao peel. The bottle contains tiny flakes of pure gold leaf. The Dutch call the liqueur Bride's Tears, as when the bottle is shaken there is a cloud of golden snow.

Irish Mist This liqueur comes from Ireland and is based on Irish whiskey and heather honey.

Izarra A French liqueur from the Pyrenees which is compounded from elder flowers and herbs which have been macerated in armagnac. *Izarra* is the Basque word for 'star' and some of the rare herbs used in its production are found only in this region. Yellow Izarra is softer and less alcoholic than the green version.

Sambuca An Italian liqueur with a high alcoholic content. The two main herbs used in its production are the witch elderbush *sambucus nigra* which gives the drink its name, and liquorice, which contributes the dominant flavour. Sometimes three coffee beans are set alight on top of the liqueur which adds a toasted flavour to the drink.

Strega This Italian liqueur has an aggressive herby flavour as it is made from over seventy herbs and barks. The name means 'witch', as the liqueur is named after the magical witch's potion that legend decreed would ensure everlasting love for any two people who tasted the liquor together.

Vieille Curé A French herbal liqueur produced in Bordeaux. It is based on a blend of cognac and armagnac and is marketed in an unusual stained glass style of bottle.

Fruit-based liqueurs

Apricot Apricot flesh is macerated in brandy and some producers enrich the apricot flavour by adding the spirit obtained from distilling the apricot kernels. It is one of the most popular fruit liqueurs and is marketed as apricot brandy or under brand names such as Abricotine or Apry.

Banana The best banana liqueurs are a clear bright yellow colour with a strong bouquet of ripe bananas. Bols have a hint of vanilla in their Crème de Banane which adds to the complexity of flavour. There are dozens of banana liqueurs available as it can be imitated synthetically, so some of them are very aggressive in flavour and aroma.

Blackberry The wide availability of blackberries means that this is the most popular of the soft berry liqueurs. Brandy that has been flavoured with blackberry juice is a liqueur with an intense fruity sweetness and a fairly low alcoholic content, whereas brandy that has been distilled from the fruit is a spirit, so although it has a fruity nose it is 40% alcohol and completely dry in flavour. The German version of this fruit spirit is Brombeergeist. Both the spirit and the liqueur have a remarkable affinity for ice cream.

Blackcurrant The most famous blackcurrant liqueurs come from Burgundy and are sold as cassis, which is the French word for blackcurrant. The fruit, which has a high vitamin C content, is macerated in spirit for about two months, then mixed with sugar and distilled to provide crème de cassis. Juice is added to give it a red-purple colour and some firms market a 'double crème', which is higher in alcohol. The best examples are thick sticky liquids with a rich fruit flavour. Cassis will take on a brownish tinge if exposed to the air for too long and cassis syrup is not a liqueur but a non-alcoholic flavouring.

Cherry Cherry liqueur is made by pressing the cherries to extract the juice, which is then mixed with brandy. Some of the stones get crushed in this process, so adding extra cherry character to the product. There are many cherry brandies available and their flavours vary according to the type of cherry used in production. For example, the Dutch firms Bols and De Kuyper both import the rich Marasca cherries from Yugoslavia, the British firm of Grants use their local morella cherries, while Cusenier's liqueur is a mixture of red cherries from Burgundy and black cherries from Alsace. Some cherry liqueurs are marketed under brand names such as Cherry Marnier, Peter Heering, Prinzenkirsch and Cheri-Suisse. Maraschino is also a cherry liqueur, although it is made by a slightly different process, as the cherries and stones are crushed, distilled and sweetened. The clear liquid has an intense cherry flavour and the most famous examples are produced in Yugoslavia and Italy from the wild sour Marasca cherry. Kirsch is distilled from fermented cherries, so is a dry spirit, not a liqueur, although it has a powerful fruit aroma.

Coconut These are fairly new liqueurs made by macerating coconut flesh in white rum. Most are sold under brand names such as Cocoribe, Malibu and RonCoco.

Mandarin The natural acid content of citrus fruits makes them excellent ingredients for liqueurs. The peels of Spanish tangerines are macerated in cognac to produce Mandarine Napoleon, and Van der Hum is a South African liqueur produced from *naartjies*, a local tangerine.

Melon Another of the new style of liqueurs. The most internationally recognized example is Midori Melon Liqueur, produced by Suntory in Japan. The musk melon gives this liqueur an exciting minty green colour and powerful aroma, but it has an unexpectedly sweet flavour.

Orange Orange liqueurs are referred to as 'curacaos', in honour of the Dutch island colony in the Caribbean that originally produced the bitter oranges used to make these liqueurs. Today there are a number of different styles of curacaos. For example, Bols market an amber coloured Dry Orange Curacao, a colourless Triple Sec, an orange coloured Bitter Orange, a Green Curacao and a Blue Curacao. Grand Marnier takes its amber colour from its cognac base and the peels of bitter oranges, while Cointreau has an assertive orange flavour but is colourless because it is based on neutral spirit. Nassau Orange, from the house of De Kuyper, is a blend of oranges and herbs and is the same liqueur that was used to toast the Dutch landing at the Cape of Good Hope over three hundred years ago. There are many other orange liqueurs such as the sweet Koum Kouat of Corfu which is produced from the tiny cumquat orange, Forbidden Fruit from the United States which has a grapefruit and orange base and Aurum, the golden brandy-based liqueur from Italy.

Peach Peaches are matured with other juices in brandy to produce this liqueur. Firms that market a range of liqueurs include a peach brandy, although most of the world's peach liqueur is made in the United States. By far the most successful is Southern Comfort, a whisky-based liqueur-spirit flavoured with peaches and oranges. The only other certainty about Southern Comfort is that it has other ingredients, as the secret recipe runs for over one hundred pages.

Pear Pear liqueurs have a rich pear nose but a subdued fruit flavour inclined to sweetness. One of the best examples is Viennese Pear from the Austrian firm of Zwack, which is made from fresh pears picked from orchards in the South Tyrol. Poire Williams is a spirit not a liqueur, as it is distilled from fermented pear juice.

Plum The sloe plum is known in France as prunelle, and this is the name of the plum liqueur that is a speciality of the Burgundy region. Some English firms still market the traditional sloe gin, produced by macerating sloe plums in sugar and gin.

Raspberry Raspberry liqueurs are especially popular in France. The soft fruit pulp is simply macerated in spirit to produce a liqueur de framboise or crème de framboise. When this liqueur is distilled, it becomes a colourless spirit known as framboise and has a powerful raspberry aroma but a completely dry taste. Cordial Campari from Italy is a raspberry liqueur with a cognac base.

Strawberry A strawberry liqueur is usually marketed under the French name of fraise or crème de fraise. If it is produced from wild strawberries, as opposed to cultivated ones, it is known as fraise de bois. Strawberry liqueur can also be distilled to make a fruit spirit and Chambéryzette is a strawberry-flavoured vermouth.

Plant- and nut-based liqueurs

Almond This liqueur is made from bitter almonds and the crushed stones of fruits. It is traditionally known as Crème de Noyau, although the most popular of today's almond liqueurs is Amaretto, which also contains apricots. The original Amaretto was produced in Saronno, Italy as early as the 16th century. Almond is the predominant flavour of Persico, a colourless sweet liqueur produced from cherries, almonds and nuts.

Anise The fruit of the anise plant is one of the oldest flavourings used by man. It has a taste very similar to liquorice, and aniseed drinks will turn cloudy when mixed with water. Alicante in Spain is acknowledged to grow the finest aniseed and this is used in the production of the best Anisette liqueurs. There are numerous aniseed drinks produced in the countries bordering the Mediterranean. The French use the word pastis to describe their aniseed drinks and the best known of these are Pernod and Ricard. Other aniseed drinks are the Greek Ouzo, Spanish Anis del Mono, Italian Elixir de China and Turkish Raki.

Caraway The German word for caraway is kummel and this is the name used to market these liqueurs. The oil of the caraway seed has long been recognized as having a calming effect on the stomach, thus the liqueur is regarded as a digestive aid. Bols were the first to market a kummel in 1575 and the company has been producing one since that date. This colourless liqueur benefits from being served on ice.

Chocolate A chocolate liqueur is flavoured with roasted cacao beans and is referred to as crème de cacao. White crème de cacao is made by simply distilling the beans, but for the brown version the beans are broken open and percolated to extract the colour before continuing the process. Chocolate marries well with other flavours, so

is used in a host of liqueurs. Chocolate Mint and Vandermint are both Dutch liqueurs, Cheri-Suisse is a chocolate-cherry combination from Switzerland, the Israeli Sabra has a chocolate-orange flavour and Afrikoko from Africa and Choclair from the U.S.A. are chocolate-coconut liqueurs. The English House of Hallgarten uses chocolate in at least eight of their liqueurs, including Royal Lemon-Chocolate and Royal Ginger-Chocolate, while Bailey's Original Irish Cream combines chocolate with cream and Irish whiskey.

Coffee Coffee beans are made from an infusion and percolation of coffee beans. They are sold under a variety of names such as coffee liqueur, crème de mocca and crème de café. Several liqueurs that are coffee flavoured are sold by brand name, including Kahlua, Tia Maria, Caffe Lolita, Bahia, Galacafe and Pasha. In addition, there are several U.S. producers of coffee-flavoured brandy.

Flower Petals Liqueurs made from flower petals need to include other ingredients to underline the flavour. The violet coloured Parfait Amour is a combination of rose petals and orange peel and has a strong flavour of vanilla, Rosolio is a reddish liqueur made from rose petals and spices, while Crème Yvette has a violet colour, perfume and flavour.

Mint Mint liqueurs are so successful because they are able to capture the tangy aroma and refreshing taste of the herb itself. The essential oil is crushed from the leaves and used to flavour the base spirit. Green crème de menthe is the most popular style, while the white version is very useful for preparing cocktails. Freezomint and Pippermint are brand names of mint liqueurs and peppermint-flavoured schnapps is produced by several U.S. firms.

Whizz Around the World

Australia

Australians take full advantage of the magnificent climate to enjoy the open air lifestyle as much as possible. Yachting, surfing and swimming are favourite outdoor sports, often combined with a casual barbecue or picnic. They were traditionally a beer-drinking nation, but wine consumption has rocketed and most homes usually keep a cask in the re-frigerator for everyday drinking. Rum from the sugar state of Queensland is one of the most popular spirits and it is often combined with tropical fruits to make long drinks.

Belgium

Belgium's geographical location in Europe means that she is able to import easily from nearby countries, so a wide range of wines, spirits and liqueurs are available there. The traditional spirit of Belgium is *genever*, the distinctively flavoured gin produced in neighbouring Holland, but the siting of the European Parliament in Brussels has meant an influx of foreign influences which have hastened the modern trend towards mixed drinks. Many of these are made with Belgium's own liqueur, the tangerine-flavoured Mandarine Napoleon.

Manly Treat

(Illustrated on page 77)

1 ms dark rum
1 ms Bols Peach Brandy
1 ms fresh lime juice
flesh of half mango
1 scoop crushed ice

Blend all the ingredients together on slow speed for 10 seconds, then pour into a medium glass filled with ice. Decorate with different coloured cocktail cherries.

Hitchhiker

1 ms Mandarine Napoleon
1 ms vodka
½ ms Campari
½ ms Bols Crème de Banane
½ ms coconut liqueur
3 ice cubes
lemonade

Blend together all except the lemonade on slow speed for 10 seconds, then pour into a tall glass filled with ice. Top up with lemonade and decorate with a slice of lime and an orange cocktail cherry.

72

Left to right: *The Running Footman, Mermaid, Fuzzhopper, The Green Man, Sweetheart Sip*

Brazil

The national drink of Brazil is Aguardente de Cana, a cane spirit similar to rum that is known locally as *cachaca*. The population are enthusiastic imbibers of *cachaca* as the annual production surpasses the entire consumption of rums in the rest of the world. The best *cachaca* will leave a froth of bubbles in the bottle if it is shaken and it is usually drunk neat, although it is also the essential ingredient of the famous Batida.

Batida Morango

(Illustrated on page 77)

2 ms cachaca
½ ms strawberry syrup
3 strawberries
1 scoop crushed ice

Blend all the ingredients together on slow speed for 5 seconds, then pour into a tall glass filled with crushed ice.

Canada

Canada is blessed with generous natural resources which stretch from the Great Lakes in the east to the Rocky Mountains in the west of this bountiful land. Canadians from Quebec to Vancouver are devotees of their local style whisky. This used to be known as 'rye' but is more correctly referred to as Canadian whisky. However, try as they might, the locals cannot outdo the Americans who consume three-quarters of Canada's production of this light-bodied mellow spirit which is an excellent mixer.

Jack Frost

(Illustrated on page 77)

2 ms Canadian whisky
½ ms Mandarine Napoleon
3 segments peeled mandarin
2 ice cubes
ginger ale

Blend together all except the ginger ale on slow speed for 10 seconds, then pour into a tall glass filled with crushed ice and top up with ginger ale. Decorate with mandarin segments.

Caribbean

Miles of white sandy beaches, crystal waters, cloudless skies, beautiful women and warm fun-filled nights make the Caribbean islands an earthly paradise for modern holidaymakers. In colonial times the abundance of sugar made these islands the birthplace of rum. Plantation owners and workers alike in Barbados, Cuba, Jamaica and Martinique would drink the fiery spirit to quench their thirst, and even now rum is still king of the Caribbean.

Fat Man's Cooler

(Illustrated on page 77)

2 ms Bacardi light rum
½ ms Bols Blue Curacao
½ ms fresh lime juice
2 ice cubes
ginger ale

Blend together the ginger ale on fast speed for 10 seconds, then pour into a tall glass filled with ice. Top up with ginger ale and decorate with a slice of lime and a red cocktail cherry. Serve with straws.

Denmark

The Danes have been drinking the colourless potent spirit known as akvavit for over 400 years. There is a ritual toast given when drinking akvavit which involves saluting one's companions with the glass, saying *skal* and drinking the liquor in one swallow, watching the other drinkers all the time. This charming habit has survived from the days when it wasn't wise to take one's eyes off the guests in case of attack.

England

The pub is the focal point for English social life and every village has at least one picturesque pub, often with a huge roaring fire to warm the locals while they stand pint in hand, chatting to neighbours. At home they usually enjoy a gin and tonic but, if guests come to call in the afternoon, they will be offered that most English of institutions, tea. The capital, London, is not only an international trading centre and a major tourist attraction, it is also the home of British Royalty, who add a touch of regal splendour to the graceful city.

Finland

Finland is a cold place as much of the country lies within the Arctic Circle and the climate dominates the lifestyle of the people. Winters are long, severely cold and very dark, but in summer, although it is still quite chilly, the daylight seems to last forever, as this is the land of the Midnight Sun. The Finns are dedicated vodka drinkers and the spirit is now one of Finland's major exports, but there are also some unusual liqueurs made from the berries which grow in the forests and marshlands.

Mermaid

(Illustrated on page 73)

1 ms akvavit
½ ms Bols Cherry Brandy
¼ ms dry vermouth
1 dash lime cordial
1 dash egg white
2 ice cubes

Blend all the ingredients together on slow speed for 10 seconds, then pour into a cocktail glass.

The Running Footman

(Illustrated on page 73)

½ ms gin
1 ms orange juice
1 slice peach
1 ice cube
champagne

Blend together all except the champagne on slow speed for 10 seconds, then pour into a champagne tulip glass and top up with cold champagne.

Lumberjack

1½ ms vodka
1 ms lemon juice
½ ms sugar syrup
6 pitted cherries
1 scoop crushed ice
soda water

Blend all the ingredients except the soda water on slow speed for 15 seconds, then pour into a tall glass filled with ice. Top up with soda water and decorate with a slice of lemon and a red cocktail cherry.

France

France is the home of some of the world's most famous beverages and each region has its own speciality. Bordeaux and Burgundy have those fabulous purple-red wines, from the sleepy town of Cognac comes one of the finest spirits, Normandy is fiercely proud of its Calvados and the perfumed white wines of Alsace are a heady delight. However, to most people France means Paris, the elegant feminine city whose night life bubbles like the delicious champagne that is produced a few kilometres away.

Germany

The Germans are a beer-drinking nation but they also appreciate the finer things of life like the light fruity wines from the Mosel and the delicate fruit brandies from the Black Forest, while their fresh cream gâteaux and tortes are imitated all over the world. Spirits are not as important as beers and wines but they do produce *wacholder*, a clear spirit similar to gin, and *weinbrand*, which is German brandy.

Crystal Fizz

(Illustrated on front cover)

½ ms Poire Williams
1 dash Bols Dry Orange Curacao
1 slice pear
champagne

Blend together all except the champagne on slow speed for 10 seconds, then pour into a tall champagne flute glass and top up with cold champagne. Decorate with a slice of pear.

Prost

(Illustrated right)

½ ms Bols Cherry Brandy
4 ms German white wine
2 maraschino cherries
1 scoop crushed ice
soda water

Blend together all except the soda water on slow speed for 10 seconds, then pour into a tall glass and top up with soda water. More crushed ice may be added if required. Decorate with a slice of lemon and a red cocktail cherry.

Left to right: *Manly Treat, Fat Man's Cooler, Geisha Girl, Sporran Opener, Prost, Jack Frost, Batida Morango*

Greece

The thought of Greece conjures up images of lazy days spent sitting in warm Mediterranean sunshine, sipping the pine flavoured retsina wine or summoning up the strength to peel one of the juice-filled oranges that grow all through the country-side. The traditional Greek aperitif is ouzo, a clean spirit with the sweet pungent flavour of aniseed. It is enjoyed in a tall glass with plenty of ice and has the unusual characteristic of turning milky white when water is added to it.

Island Sun

1 ms ouzo
¼ thin-skinned orange
3 dashes grenadine
2 ice cubes

Blend all the ingredients together, including the unpeeled orange, on slow speed for 15 seconds, then pour into a tall glass filled with ice.

Hawaii

Hawaii is different! The sun shines brighter, the air smells fresher, the surf rolls higher and happiness is everywhere, for this is the tourist Mecca of America. Sugar is big business as well, so it is not surprising that there is a thriving light rum industry and the islands produce a unique spirit known as Okolehao, known locally as 'oke', which is derived from the roots of the ti plant. Both rum and oke are used extensively in many bars on the islands to mix a range of exotic cocktails featuring the local tropical fruits.

Surfside Swinger

1 ms light rum
1 ms gin
flesh of passionfruit
4 cubes pineapple
1 dash grenadine
2 ice cubes

Blend all the ingredients together on slow speed for 15 seconds, then pour into a tiki bowl or large glass filled with ice and slices of fruit. Serve with straws.

Holland

The Dutch take their social drinking very seriously and fill the thousands of cafés late into the night. Holland is the home of liqueurs and Dutch liqueurs have had an international reputation for hundreds of years. In Holland liqueurs are traditionally served in a small glass full to the brim, so that the drinker must lean over and take a sip while the glass is still on the bar. Also, the Dutch have a great fondness for the locally produced advocaat, a creamy blend of egg yolks and brandy which is so thick it can be eaten with a spoon.

Fuzzhopper

(Illustrated on page 73)

1 ms brandy
½ ms Bols Advocaat
½ ms Bols Peach Brandy
flesh of half peach
1 dash lime cordial
lemonade

Blend together all except the lemonade on fast speed for 7 seconds, then pour into a tall glass filled with ice. Splash lemonade on top and decorate with a slice of orange and a red cocktail cherry.

Hong Kong

In Hong Kong, East and West meld together to produce a unique panorama. Office blocks and apartments tower over thousands of houseboats anchored in the bays, European restaurants and street sellers compete for the same customers, and tourists jostle in the market place with Chinese women bargaining for the day's food. Hong Kong is one of the world's leading money markets, so much hard bargaining is also done around the boardroom tables. Residents have adopted brandy as their drink to such a degree that Hong Kong is now one of the main export markets for cognac.

Taipan

2 ms brandy
1 ms Bols Apricot Brandy
1 ms mango nectar
4 cubes papaya
1 scoop crushed ice

Blend all the ingredients together on slow speed for 20 seconds, then pour into a medium-size glass. Decorate with coloured cocktail cherries.

Ireland

The 'Emerald Isle' is a timeless land of gentle hills, soft mists and green pastures peopled by a warm-hearted race steeped in folklore and song. This is the nation that invented whiskey and the Irish have been distilling their own full-bodied bracing spirit for over 800 years.

Legend has it that they stole the recipe for beer from England, but managed to burn the barley before perfecting the brew, and so was born Guinness, the stout that has become the world's most identifiable product of Ireland.

The Green Man

(Illustrated on page 73)

1 ms Irish whiskey
½ ms Bols Blue Curacao
1 ms fresh lemon juice
1 dash egg white
3 ice cubes

Blend all the ingredients together on slow speed for 10 seconds, then pour into a medium-size glass filled with ice.

Italy

Italy is known as the world's largest wine producer, but it also makes an amazing range of other alcoholic beverages as there are many towns producing a local speciality which may be a bitters, a liqueur or a special aperitif. Some of these are internationally famous – vermouth from Turin, Campari from Milan, amaretto from Saronno, Strega from Benevento – while others are known only within a small radius of the centre of production.

Sweetheart Sip

(Illustrated on page 73)

1 ms vodka
½ ms Amaretto di Saronno
½ ms vermouth bianco
flesh of half peach
3 ice cubes

Blend all the ingredients together on slow speed for 10 seconds, then pour into a large cocktail glass.

Japan

Japan is a kaleidoscope of ancient tradition and modern culture. Images of geisha girls and tea ceremonies still linger with many Westerners, but 20th-century Japan is also big business and heavy industry, and while a Japanese woman still wears a kimono at home, she goes out dressed in the latest French fashion. More whisky is now consumed in Japan than the traditional *sake* and a liqueur industry is developing with products such as Midori achieving international recognition.

Geisha Girl

(Illustrated on page 77)

1 ms Midori Melon Liqueur
1 ms gin
2 ms passionfruit nectar
flesh of half pear
3 ice cubes

Blend all the ingredients together on slow speed for 10 seconds, then pour into a medium-size glass filled with ice. Decorate with black grapes.

New Zealand

Each of the two islands that form New Zealand has its own character. The North Island is a beautiful green pastureland formed by rolling hills while the South Island is a majestic sweep of mountains, so the country is often covered with a gentle mist which inspired the Maori name for their home, 'Land of the Long White Cloud'. The volcanic origins of the land are very obvious as there are numerous hot springs, geysers and crater lakes which are an added attraction for the holiday-makers who take advantage of the ski slopes near the winter holiday resorts.

Kiwi Cooler

2 ms light rum
½ ms Midori
2 ms grapefruit juice
2 peeled Kiwi fruit
2 scoops crushed ice

Blend all the ingredients together on slow speed for 20 seconds, then pour into a large glass. Decorate with kiwi slices and serve with straws.

Portugal

Portugal is a land of stark contrast between old and new. Fast cars zoom past donkeys laden with firewood, black-clad women sit motionless in doorways and gypsies do their washing in the rivers just a few miles from the modern multi-storey hotels. Portugal is most famous for her port which begins its life in the piercing heat of the mountain vineyards and matures in the cool coastal Lodges of Oporto – however, the local people are more partial to the fiery brandy-like spirit known as aguadente.

Santa Maria

1 ms aguadente
1 ms triple sec
1 ms lemon juice
3 ice cubes

Blend all the ingredients together on fast speed for 10 seconds, then pour into a cocktail glass.

Scotland

The scenic beauty of Scotland attracts many thousands of tourists every year and the offshore oil discoveries have brought a new aspect to life there. However, the product that has made Scotland internationally famous is her whisky, because 'Scotch', said with a faint air of reverence, is asked for in virtually every bar in the world. Scotland is blessed with the purest of water to make her whisky, the peat to flavour it and the Highland mist to mature it to perfection.

Sporran Opener

(Illustrated on page 77)

1½ ms Scotch whisky
½ ms Bols Apricot Brandy
1 ms orange juice
1 dash Angostura bitters
2 ice cubes

Blend all the ingredients together on slow speed for 10 seconds, then pour into a medium-size glass filled with crushed ice.

South Africa

South Africa's geographical location at the southernmost tip of the African continent meant that it was a natural port of call for traders using the sea routes from Europe to the Far East and people of many different nationalities have settled there. It is a magnificent land, quite green and fertile around the coastline where Cape Town is the main focus of activity, but stretching back into the high plains that may not see rain for years at a time. South Africa has a thriving wine industry and produces very high quality brandy. There is also a unique local liqueur made from tangerines named Van der Hum.

Diamond Ice

2 ms brandy
1 ms Van der Hum
1 ms sugar syrup
4 grapefruit segments
1 scoop crushed ice

Blend all the ingredients together on slow speed for 20 seconds, then pour into a medium-size glass filled with ice. Serve with straws.

Spain

Spain's wide beaches and long hours of sunshine have made it one of Europe's most popular tourist resorts. The south of Spain is sherry country and the vines grow for miles around the stately old town of Jerez where the strong golden wine has been produced for centuries. The country has a flourishing wine industry and is building a reputation for good sparkling wine, so it is something of a paradox that the Spanish are very big consumers of brandy.

Sherry Whizz

1 ms dry sherry
½ ms whisky
1 ms orange juice
2 dashes Bols Dry Orange Curacao
1 dash egg white
2 ice cubes

Blend all the ingredients together on slow speed for 10 seconds, then pour into a medium-size glass.

Switzerland

Switzerland's greatest assets are the mountains. They provide her with rich pasture land, a defence barrier in times of attack and the most magnificent skiing slopes that attract skiers from all over the world. The mountain resorts are companionable places in the evenings, with roaring fires, cheese fondues and numerous glasses of Switzerland's special fruit brandies which are distilled from plums, cherries and pears that grow in profusion in the alpine valleys.

Cherry Silk

(Illustrated on page 6)

1 ms Cheri-Suisse
1 ms brandy
2 maraschino cherries
1 scoop vanilla ice cream
2 ice cubes

Blend all the ingredients together on slow speed for 10 seconds, then pour into a sundae glass. Decorate with a cherry.

United States

The United States is a land of contrast, encompassing people of many cultures and a diversity of lifestyles. However, there is some essential element that reaches from New York to Dallas and San Francisco and binds them all together as a nation. Americans have a unique way of making something their own. They have elevated breakfast to the level of a social event, have adopted turkey and cranberry sauce as a national dish and treasure the cocktail as a truly American invention.

Preservation Tipple

1 ms Southern Comfort
½ ms orange juice
½ ms fresh lemon juice
flesh of half mango
1 dash Pernod
1 dash egg white
1 scoop crushed ice

Blend all the ingredients together on slow speed for 10 seconds, then pour into a tall glass and decorate with a sprig of fresh mint.

U.S.S.R.

Russia is a Union of many different races and cultures as diverse as the Cossacks of the Black Sea to the Mongols of the eastern seaboard. Essentially it is an agricultural country where long severe winters freeze the soil and restrict travel, while Moscow is an imposing city where the nationalities combine to fill the numerous government offices. Wherever they live, Russians drink vodka. The frozen neat spirit is taken in one swallow, which has the effect of warming the drinker very quickly, and on special occasions the glass is smashed afterwards to bring luck to the celebration.

Frozen Zing

2 ms vodka
1 ms lemon juice
1 scoop crushed ice

Blend all the ingredients together on fast speed for 10 seconds, then pour into a chilled cocktail glass. Add a twist of lemon peel.

TEQUILA: *the sunshine spirit*

Tequila! The word conjures up images of desert, shimmering heat, sombreros and siestas, for tequila is the essence of Mexico. The Mexicans still drink it in the traditional way, which is something of a test for the uninitiated because of its ritual aspect, not to mention the impact on the palate. Firstly, a Mexican moistens the base of his thumb and sprinkles salt on it. A small glass of neat tequila is held between the thumb and the forefinger and a wedge of lime between the forefinger and the middle finger. Then in quick succession he licks the salt, downs the tequila and bites into the lime. The taste sensation is something akin to swallowing a lighted fire cracker, and it is guaranteed to bring a blush of colour to the cheeks of even the heartiest soul and probably a tear to the eye as well. Tequila, it seems, is many things to many people. In Mexico it is thought to cure dysentery and calm a nursing baby, whilst it is also popular as an after-shave lotion, a disinfectant and a love potion!

Although the spirit has been distilled in Mexico since the 1500s, it was not until the early 1970s that its popularity spread to the U.S.A. via the university campuses, where tequila was identified as the new spirit for the new generation. Then, whilst on tour in America in 1972, the Rolling Stones became fond of a tequila cocktail and the Tequila Sunrise was in worldwide demand overnight. Sales of the spirit have increased steadily ever since, with the majority of tequila drinkers aged between eighteen and thirty-four.

The agave plant resembles a cactus and for thousands of years it was used by the Indian civilizations to provide food, cloth, paper and thread. Also, the sharp spikes could be used as needles or for slipping under the enemy's fingernails. The juice of the plant was fermented into a milky alcoholic liquid known as pulque. In ancient times pulque was regarded as sacred and drunkenness was rewarded by the death penalty. However, all that changed when the Spanish invaders arrived and used their knowledge to distil a spirit known as mezcal from the plant. Mezcal's main claim to fame seems to be its ability to drown a worm, as there is a dead one in most bottles. Any plausible reason for this defies imagination: Is it a warning? A flavour additive? A snack?

There are more than 400 species of agave plants and the one known as the 'blue' variety yields a superior spirit to all other species. For this reason the drink is given another name, tequila, after the town of the same name that lies in the heart of the blue agave territory. Thus, while tequila is mezcal, not all mezcal is tequila. Tequila must come from the blue agave plant that has been grown in a delineated region of Mexico to earn the official government stamp of authenticity.

It takes the spiky plant about ten years to reach maturity, by which time its fruit is like a giant pine cone about 25 inches (64 cm) in diameter. The fruit is harvested by hand, then cooked to a soft pulp that is shredded and milled to extract the juice. The juice is then fermented with yeast and cane sugar before being double distilled in a pot still and filtered through charcoal to produce the clear spirit sold as tequila. Often this is referred to as white or silver tequila, whilst gold tequila has an amber colour due to ageing in oak barrels that have previously held bourbon or brandy.

The two biggest tequila-producing families – known as tequileros – are Cuervo and Sauza, and in the Latin style a blood feud over a woman has existed between them in past generations. It ended with a marriage between the two tequileros, so today they battle it out with sales figures for the largest share of the world tequila market.

Shaken and Stirred

Shaken

A drink is shaken when the ingredients need thorough mixing to amalgamate them. Traditionally, recipes containing fruit juices, syrups and dairy products required the vigorous action of the cocktail shaker. Also, plenty of ice is used whilst shaking to ensure that the drink is chilled properly.

Barbican

2 ms Scotch whisky
¼ ms Drambuie
½ ms passionfruit nectar

Shake with ice and strain into a cocktail glass.

Bosom Caresser

1½ ms brandy
½ ms Bols Dry Orange Curacao
1 egg yolk
2 dashes grenadine

Shake with ice and strain into a medium-size glass.

Bullshot

(Illustrated opposite)

1 ms vodka
2 ms beef bouillon
1 dash fresh lemon juice
2 dashes Worcestershire sauce
celery salt

Shake with ice and strain into a medium-size glass.

Ghannam Pink

1 ms vodka
2 ms grapefruit juice
½ ms Campari
1 dash sugar syrup
egg white

Shake with ice and strain into a medium-size glass.

Golden Medallion

1 ms brandy
1 ms Galliano
1 ms orange juice
1 dash egg white

Shake with ice and strain into a cocktail glass. Add a twist of orange rind on top.

Left to right: *Singapore Sling, Bullshot, Old Fashioned, Tigertini, White Lady*

Mary Pickford

1½ ms light rum
1½ ms pineapple juice
2 dashes grenadine
1 dash Bols Maraschino

Shake with ice and strain into a cocktail glass.

Mint Royal

1 ms brandy
1 ms Bols Chocolate Mint
1 ms fresh lemon juice
1 dash egg white

Shake with ice and strain into a cocktail glass.

Singapore Sling

(Illustrated on page 85)

2 ms gin
1 ms Bols Cherry Brandy
1 ms fresh lemon juice
½ ms sugar syrup
soda water

Shake all the ingredients except the soda water with ice and strain into a tall glass filled with ice. Top up with soda water and decorate with slices of lemon and a cocktail cherry. Serve with straws.

Whisky Sour

2 ms whisky
2 ms fresh lemon juice
½ ms sugar syrup
1 dash egg white

Shake with ice and strain into a medium-size glass. Decorate with a slice of lemon.
   Other spirits or liqueurs can be substituted for the whisky.

Stirred

A drink is stirred so that it can be served cold and ingredients that only need a gentle stir to blend together are mixed in a mixing glass with plenty of ice. Sometimes the glass in which the drink is served becomes a miniature mixing glass because the ingredients are stirred through the ice to chill the drink before it is served.

Brandy Crusta

(Illustrated on page 15)

1 ms brandy
½ ms Bols Dry Orange Curacao
3 dashes Bols Maraschino
1 dash Angostura bitters
2 dashes fresh lemon juice

Rub the rim of a medium-size glass with lemon and dip it into sugar. Fit a complete spiral of orange peel into the glass and fill with ice.
   Stir all ingredients with ice in a mixing glass and strain into prepared glass. Add a cocktail cherry.
   A crusta can be made with any spirit.

Dandy

1 ms Canadian whisky
1 ms Dubonnet
3 dashes triple sec
1 dash Angostura bitters

Stir with ice and strain into a cocktail glass. Decorate with twists of orange and lemon.

Gimlet

1½ ms gin
½ ms lime cordial

Stir with ice in a mixing glass and strain into a medium-size glass filled with ice. Add a splash of soda water if desired.

Hunter

1½ ms Jack Daniels
½ ms Bols Cherry Brandy

Stir with ice in a mixing glass and strain into a cocktail glass.

Mint Julep

2 ms Jack Daniels
1 ms sugar syrup
6 mint leaves

Muddle the sugar and mint until thick, then put the mixture into a medium-size glass and leave in the refrigerator until cold. Then fill with ice and pour in Jack Daniels.

Stir very gently so that the mixture does not cloud. Decorate with a sprig of fresh mint.

Negroni

1 ms gin
½ ms sweet vermouth
½ ms Campari

Fill a medium-size glass with ice and pour in the ingredients. Stir gently until cold and drop in a slice of orange.

Old Fashioned

(Illustrated on page 85)

2 ms Canadian whisky
1 ms sugar syrup
2 dashes Angostura bitters

Put the sugar and Angostura into an old-fashioned whisky glass and fill with ice. Pour in Canadian whisky and stir gently, then drop in two slices of orange and a red cocktail cherry. Serve with a stirrer.

Tequila Sunrise

2 ms tequila
4 ms orange juice
½ ms grenadine

Fill a tall glass with ice and pour in tequila and orange juice. Stir until the mixture is very cold then splash grenadine on top. Decorate with a slice of orange and a red cocktail cherry. Serve with straws.

Tom Collins

1½ ms gin
1 ms fresh lemon juice
½ ms sugar syrup
1 dash Angostura bitters
soda water

Fill a tall glass with ice and pour in the lemon juice, gin and sugar. Top up with soda water, stirring vigorously as you do so. Splash the Angostura on top and drop in a slice of lemon.

New York, New York!

Bronx

1½ ms gin
½ ms dry vermouth
½ ms sweet vermouth
½ ms orange juice
1 dash egg white

Shake all ingredients with ice and strain into a cocktail glass.

Left to right: *Bronx, Manhattan on-the-Rocks, Manhattan, New Yorker, Brooklyn, Fifth Avenue*

Manhattan

2 ms Canadian whisky
1 ms sweet vermouth
1 dash Angostura bitters

Stir all ingredients in a mixing glass and strain into a cocktail glass or into a medium-size glass filled with ice. Add a red cocktail cherry.

New Yorker

2 ms Jack Daniels
½ ms fresh lime juice
½ ms grenadine

Shake all ingredients with ice and strain into a cocktail glass. Add a twist of orange rind.

Brooklyn

1 ms Canadian whisky
1 ms sweet vermouth
1 dash Bols Maraschino
1 dash Amer Picon

Stir with ice in a mixing glass and strain into a cocktail glass.

Fifth Avenue

1 ms Bols brown Crème de Cacao
1 ms Bols Apricot Brandy
1 ms cream

Pour ingredients in order given into a straight-sided liqueur glass, taking care that each floats on top of another.

Martinis

The Martini is the Western world's equivalent to the iced vodka enjoyed by the Russians and Poles and the akvavit the Danes drink straight from the freezer. It is virtually neat spirit served ice cold and is meant to be sipped slowly. The herb flavourings in the vermouth contribute a touch of complexity to the spirit and the final touch of oil from the rind of lemon or olive skin adds to the subtle taste sensation.

Dry Martini Cocktail

2 ms gin
2 dashes dry vermouth

Stir with ice in a mixing glass or large jug and strain into a cocktail glass. Ice may be served in the drink if desired. Add a twist of lemon rind or an olive.

Gibson

(Illustrated on page 15)

2 ms gin
1 dash dry vermouth

Stir with ice in a mixing glass or large jug and strain into a cocktail glass. Ice may be served in the drink if desired. Add a cocktail onion.

Fleurtini

2 ms gin
2 dashes orange flower water

Stir with ice in a mixing glass or large jug and strain into a cocktail glass. Ice may be served in the drink if desired. Rub the rim of the glass with a piece of orange peel before tasting.

Perfect Martini

2 ms gin
2 dashes dry vermouth
2 dashes sweet vermouth

Stir with ice in a mixing glass or large jug and strain into a cocktail glass. Ice may be served in the drink if desired. A twist of lemon rind or a red cocktail cherry is optional.

Sakatini

2 ms gin
2 dashes sake

Stir with ice in a mixing glass or large jug and strain into a cocktail glass. Ice may be served in the drink if desired. Add an olive.

Sweet Martini Cocktail

1½ ms gin
½ ms sweet vermouth

Stir with ice in a mixing glass or large jug and strain into a cocktail glass. Ice may be served in the drink if desired. Add a red cocktail cherry.

Tigertini

(Illustrated on page 85)

1½ ms gin
½ ms rosé vermouth

Stir with ice in a mixing glass or large jug and strain into a cocktail glass. Ice may be served in the drink if desired. Add a twist of orange rind.

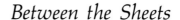

Vodkatini

2 ms vodka
2 dashes dry vermouth

Stir with ice in a mixing glass or large jug and strain into a cocktail glass. Ice may be served in the drink if desired. Add a twist of lemon rind or an olive.

Wet Martini

2 ms tequila
2 dashes dry vermouth
salt

Rim the edge of a martini glass by rubbing it with lemon, then dipping it in salt. Stir the tequila and vermouth with ice in a mixing glass and strain it into the prepared glass.

Oranges and Lemons

Orange liqueur and fresh lemon juice produce one of the most successful flavour combinations in the cocktail spectrum as the liqueur contributes not only an orange taste but also enough sweetness to balance the sharp citrus tang of the lemon juice. Each spirit adds its own character to the orange-lemon flavour, so a range of drinks can be easily produced by simply varying the spirit.

Balalaika

1 ms vodka
1 ms Cointreau
1 ms fresh lemon juice
1 dash egg white

Shake all the ingredients together with ice and strain into a cocktail glass. A cocktail cherry is optional.

Between the Sheets

1 ms brandy
1 ms light rum
1 ms triple sec
2 dashes fresh lemon juice

Shake all the ingredients together with ice and strain into a cocktail glass.

Bullfrog

1 ms dry vermouth
1 ms triple sec
1 ms lemon juice

Shake all the ingredients together with ice and strain into a cocktail glass. Decorate with a silver parasol, green cocktail cherries and straws.

Firefly

1 ms gin
½ ms tequila
½ ms Bols Dry Orange Curacao
½ ms lemon juice
dash egg white

Shake all the ingredients together with ice and strain into a cocktail glass. Add a twist of lemon.

Pink Lady

1 ms gin
1 ms Cointreau
1 ms lemon juice
½ ms grenadine
1 dash egg white

Shake all the ingredients together with ice and strain into a cocktail glass.

Sidecar

1 ms brandy
1 ms Cointreau
1 ms fresh lemon juice

Shake all the ingredients together with ice and strain into a cocktail glass.

Silent Third

1 ms Scotch whisky
1 ms triple sec
1 ms fresh lemon juice

Shake all the ingredients together with ice and strain into a cocktail glass.

Tongue Twister

1 ms light rum
½ ms Malibu
½ ms Bols Dry Orange Curacao
1 ms lemon juice

Shake all the ingredients together with ice and strain into a cocktail glass.

Torpedo

1 ms tequila
1 ms Bols Dry Orange Curacao
1 ms fresh lemon juice
1 dash egg white

Shake all the ingredients together with ice and strain into a cocktail glass. Add a twist of lemon rind on top.

White Lady

(Illustrated on page 85)

1 ms gin
1 ms Cointreau
1 ms fresh lemon juice
1 dash egg white

Shake all the ingredients together with ice and strain into a cocktail glass. Add a red cocktail cherry.

X.Y.Z.

1 ms golden rum
1ms triple sec
1 ms fresh lemon juice

Shake all the ingredients together with ice and strain into a cocktail glass.

Zip Fastener

1 ms dark rum
1ms Bols Dry Orange Curacao
½ ms Bols Coffee Liqueur
1 ms fresh lemon juice

Shake all the ingredients together with ice and strain into a cocktail glass.

VERMOUTH: *treasure from the Alps*

Vermouth is wine that has been flavoured with herbs and spices, and it is not a coincidence that the companies producing it have their distilleries close to the French and Italian Alps, as it is in this alpine region that the plants and flowers used in vermouth production flourish best.

A style of vermouth was the first 'mixed' drink ever invented, as the Egyptians are known to have spiced wine with honey, frankincense, juniper berries and lotus leaves, whilst the Romans blended wine with flower blossoms and honey. This habit probably came about as wine was stored in huge stone jars which were not airtight, so the wine turned sour very quickly and the herb-spice mixture would disguise the unpleasant taste. In ancient times these spiced wines were more of a necessity than a luxury, not only because water was usually unsafe to drink, but also because food was often in a state of deterioration, preservatives being virtually unknown. The early physicians actively promoted the use of spiced wine as bitter medicines could be dissolved in it, and the wine itself contained valuable health properties. This medicinal use of the beverage continued into the Middle Ages, when healing became the province of monks, so that recipes were passed from monastery to monastery and the reputation of herb-spice wine was known throughout Europe.

One of the ingredients that has been used to flavour wine since the earliest times has the botanical name *Artemisia absinthium*, known in English as wormwood, and the modern word vermouth is derived from the German translation *wermut*. Today, only the flowers of the wormwood are used in vermouth production as it is prohibited to use the leaves which contain a substance known to induce a state of stupor. It was the 'absinthe' made from wormwood leaves that was so popular with the poor of Paris in the 19th century. As many as fifty different ingredients are used to flavour some brands of vermouth and the companies guard their recipes closely. Much of the bitterness comes from the bark of the quinine tree and bitter orange peel while camomile, coriander, mint, cinnamon, sage, thyme, orris, rose leaves and angelica are some of the other flavourings.

The two giants of the vermouth industry are Martini & Rossi and Cinzano, both of which have their headquarters in Turin, Italy, whilst Noilly Prat is the most well known of the French firms.

Bitter-Sweet Success

Some of the most useful ingredients in cocktail mixing are 'bitters' which have a style and flavour all their own. Essentially, they are essences of herbs, bark and spices, but the flavour is so concentrated that brands such as Underberg are sold in miniature-sized bottles. However, they are still quite alcoholic, many of them being over 40% alcohol by volume.

Italians are very fond of bitters and drink them neat out of small glasses, over ice or topped up with soda. One of the most popular brands is Cynar, made from an essence of artichokes. Supposedly containing a substance that exerts a calming influence, Cynar is also taken before bedtime with hot water, lemon peel and sugar. Another Italian success story is Fernet Branca. Some believe this black syrupy liquid is an aphrodisiac but most take it as an appetite sharpener before lunch, while elsewhere in the world it is drunk by hopeful souls who believe it can cure hangovers.

Softly Softly

Non-Alcoholic

Amelia

(Illustrated opposite)

2 ms orange juice
1 ms blackcurrant cordial
10 pineapple cubes
2 ice cubes

Blend together all except the blackcurrant cordial on slow speed for 10 seconds, then pour into a tall glass filled with ice. Splash blackcurrant cordial on top just before serving. Serve with straws.

Angel's Milk

2 ms peach nectar
4 ms cold milk
½ ms orgeat syrup
1 egg
2 ice cubes

Blend all the ingredients together on fast speed for 10 seconds, then pour into a large bowl-type glass.

Babywalker

2 drinks

10 ms cold milk
12 strawberries
flesh of ½ avocado
1 ms fresh lemon juice

Blend all the ingredients together on slow speed for 15 seconds, then pour into tall glasses. Decorate with a strawberry.

Bananalui

1 ms cream
2 ms passionfruit nectar
1 banana
1 scoop ice

Blend all the ingredients together on slow speed for 10 seconds, then pour into a large glass.

Cocomint

2 ms grapefruit juice
2 ms pineapple juice
1 ms coconut cream
½ ms peppermint cordial

Blend all the ingredients together on fast speed for 7 seconds, then pour into a tall glass filled with ice.

Left to right: *Pussyfruit, Amelia, Pinta Colada, Avalanche, Cherry Froth*

Fizzgig

2 scoops vanilla ice cream
1 ms lime cordial
Coca-Cola

Blend the ice cream and lime cordial on slow speed for 5 seconds, then pour into a large glass and fill up with Coca-Cola. Decorate with fruit and serve with straws.

Grapefruit Cooler

4 ms cold milk
1 scoop vanilla ice cream
1 grapefruit
6 mint leaves
1 scoop crushed ice

Peel the grapefruit then cut it into small pieces and put them into the blender jug with the other ingredients.

Blend on slow speed for 20 seconds, then pour into a sundae glass. Decorate with a wedge of grapefruit and fresh mint.

Lazy Milktaker

4 ms cold milk
1 ms grenadine
12 raspberries
1 banana
3 ice cubes

Blend all the ingredients together on slow speed for 10 seconds, then pour into a tall glass. Serve with straws.

Miri-Belle

3 ms cold milk
1 ms coconut cream
2 scoops vanilla ice cream
1 dash grenadine

Blend all the ingredients together on slow speed for 10 seconds, then pour into a tall glass.

Morning Call

4 ms pineapple juice
1 ms lime cordial
1 peach
2 ice cubes
grenadine

Blend together all except the grenadine on fast speed for 10 seconds, then pour into a tall glass filled with ice. Splash grenadine on top.

Orange Flip

8 tablespoons plain yoghurt
1 orange
1 ms orange squash
1 egg
3 ice cubes

Blend all the ingredients together on high speed for 10 seconds, then pour into a tall glass.

Pinta Colada

(Illustrated on page 95)

6 ms cold milk
4 ms pineapple juice
1 ms coconut cream
2 ice cubes

Blend all the ingredients together on fast speed for 10 seconds, then pour into a large glass filled with ice. Decorate with a slice of pineapple and serve with straws.

Pussyfruit

(Illustrated on page 95)

6 pineapple chunks
3 strawberries
½ peach
2 ms orange juice
2 ms lemon juice
1 dash grenadine
1 egg
1 scoop crushed ice

Blend all the ingredients together on slow speed for 10 seconds, then pour into a large glass. Decorate with slices of fruit and cocktail cherries. Serve with straws.

Red Devil

6 ms tomato juice
1 egg
3 dashes Tabasco sauce
freshly ground pepper

Blend all the ingredients together on slow speed for 10 seconds, then pour into a tall glass filled with ice.

Tenderberry

1 ms grenadine
1 ms cream
6 strawberries
ginger ale

Blend together all except the ginger ale on fast speed for 10 seconds, then pour into a large glass filled with ice. Top up with ginger ale and sprinkle ground ginger on top.

Lightly Alcoholic

Apple Pie

1 ms sweet vermouth
3 ms apple juice
½ ms lime cordial
1 scoop crushed ice
soda water

Blend together all except the soda water on fast speed for 10 seconds. Pour into a tall glass and top up with soda water.

Candyfloss

3 ms white wine
12 raspberries
1 dash lemon squash
1 dash egg white
1 scoop crushed ice
soda water

Blend together all except the soda water on slow speed for 10 seconds. Pour into a large glass and top up with soda water.

Frou Frou

(Illustrated on page 99)

1 ms Bols Advocaat
½ banana
1 scoop crushed ice
lemonade

Blend together all except the lemonade on slow speed for 10 seconds. Pour into a medium-size glass and top up with lemonade.

Left to right: *Kir Sherbet, Mahogany, Nell Gwynn, Frou Frou*

Kir Sherbet

(Illustrated on page 99)

4 ms dry white wine
1 ms crème de cassis
1 scoop crushed ice

Blend all the ingredients together on slow speed until smooth, then pour into a large wine glass.

Mahogany

(Illustrated on page 99)

1 ms Bols Coffee Liqueur
Coca-Cola

Pour Bols Coffee Liqueur into a tall glass filled with ice and top up with Coca-Cola.

Nell Gwynn

(Illustrated on page 99)

1 ms Bols Apricot Brandy
2 ms orange juice

Pour both ingredients into an old-fashioned glass filled with crushed ice.

Royal Flush

1 ms Bols Cherry Brandy
dry ginger ale

Pour Bols Cherry Brandy into a tall glass filled with ice and top up with dry ginger ale.

Snowball

(Illustrated on page 15)

2 ms Bols Advocaat
1 ms lime cordial
lemonade

Pour advocaat and lime into a medium-size goblet and top up with lemonade. Decorate with a slice of orange and a red cocktail cherry.

Tropique

1 ms Bols Crème de Banane
4 ms grapefruit juice

Pour both ingredients into a tall glass filled with ice.

Watermelon Murphy

4 ms dry white wine
1 dash grenadine
4 cubes watermelon
1 scoop crushed ice

Blend all the ingredients together on slow speed for 15 seconds, then pour into a tall glass filled with ice. Decorate with a cube of watermelon on a cocktail stick.

VODKA: *a revolutionary drink*

Although vodka has been distilled in Eastern Europe for over one thousand years, it is only since the 1940s that it has achieved worldwide acclaim. However, vodka's rise to popularity in the Western world must rate as the success story of the post-war liquor industry.

Both the Poles and the Russians lay claim to having invented vodka and it has certainly existed in Eastern Europe since the 10th century, making it one of the oldest drinks known to man. The name is derived from the Russian word *woda* meaning water and in 10th century Russia there existed a honey-vodka tax. The spirit was referred to as bread wine as it was made from wheat, or as hot wine, probably because of the taste sensation of the raw spirit.

The Russian revolution was indirectly responsible for the present-day position of vodka. Thousands of people left the country during the revolution, so creating a demand for vodka in Western Europe. Members of distilling families were amongst the exiles, most notably the Smirnoffs, who had taken with them the formula for their vodka. Production was begun first in Paris, then in the U.S.A. in the 1930s. At first, sales were low as Americans found it strange to drink a spirit neat, ice cold and in one swallow. The firm that had bought the worldwide rights to Smirnoff, a family concern called Hublein, decided to try to boost sales by promoting a mixed drink featuring vodka. One correspondent wrote from the U.S.A. in 1947: 'There is a crazy concoction sweeping the West . . . it is a drink served in a copper like mug inscribed on the outside Moscow Mule. . . .' The result of similar aggressive marketing over the next two decades was an astounding increase in sales until in 1975 vodka had the major share of the spirit market, even outselling bourbon in the U.S.A., and Hublein became one of the giants of the liquor business. It is estimated that Smirnoff now sells a case of vodka for every second of the year and that there are now over 200 different brands of vodka on sale in the U.S.A. alone.

The vodkas of eastern Europe have a definite bouquet and are much more oily than the 'western' vodkas which have virtually no taste. Products such as Russia's Stolichnaya, Poland's Wyborowa and Finland's Finlandia vodkas are best drunk in the traditional manner, served ice cold in a one shot glass as they are generally stronger and have more flavour.

Schnapps

Schnapps is a general name for a white spirit similar to vodka which is widely distilled from grain or potatoes in Northern Europe. The word means 'gasp' which is an accurate description of the effect the liquor has when it is taken in one swallow. It is called in Scandinavia *akvavit* (aquavit). The Danes have been distilling it for over 400 years and have been so inordinately attached to the spirit in the past that in the late 1500s King Christian IV had to prohibit the clergy from delivering their sermons with a glass in hand. It seems this was one of a series of ineffective measures to reduce drinking, so he decided on another course of action and discovered that most effective of deterrents – taxation. Traditionally, akvavit is served neat, ice cold from the freezer, in small one shot glasses.

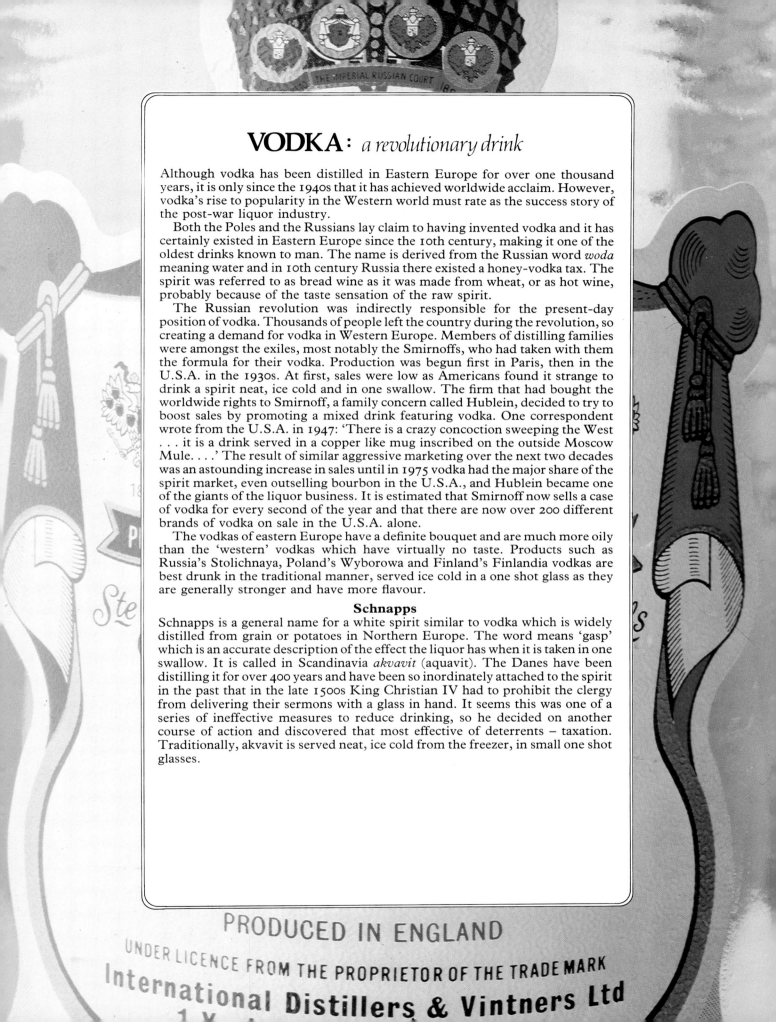

Late Night Lovelies

Anisette Cocktail

1 ms Bols Anisette
1 dash sugar syrup
1 dash Angostura bitters
1 scoop crushed ice

Blend all the ingredients together on slow speed for 5 seconds, then pour into a medium-size glass and add a splash of water. Add a twist of lemon on top.

Avalanche

(Illustrated on page 95)

1 ms amaretto
½ ms Bols Apricot Brandy
1 ms apricot nectar
1 scoop ice cream

Blend all the ingredients together on slow speed until smooth, then pour into a medium-size glass.

Cherry Froth

(Illustrated on page 95)

1 ms Bols Cherry Brandy
2 ms pineapple juice
¼ ms Bols Kirsch
4 maraschino cherries
1 egg white
1 scoop crushed ice

Blend all the ingredients together on slow speed for 10 seconds, then pour into a tall glass filled with crushed ice.

Envy

2 ms Bols Coffee Liqueur
2 ms cream
¼ ms Bols green Crème de Menthe

Pour the coffee liqueur into a small goblet. Whip together the cream and crème de menthe until thick, then spoon on top of the liqueur so that it floats.

Frostbite

1 ms tequila
½ ms Bols Blue Curacao
½ ms Bols white Crème de Cacao
2 ms cream
2 ice cubes

Blend all the ingredients together on slow speed for 10 seconds, then pour into a medium-size glass.

Frozen Comfort

1½ ms Southern Comfort
½ ms Bols Maraschino
1 ms fresh lemon juice
½ ms sugar syrup
1 scoop crushed ice

Blend all the ingredients together on slow speed for 10 seconds, then pour into a medium-size glass.

Right: *Sticky Green*

Frozen Medallion

(Illustrated on page 15)

1 ms brandy
1 ms Galliano
1 ms orange juice
1 scoop crushed ice

Blend all the ingredients together on slow speed until smooth, then pour into a small glass. Add a twist of lemon peel on top.

London Sunset

1 ms brandy
1 ms Bols Cherry Brandy
2 strawberries
champagne

Blend together all except the champagne on slow speed for 10 seconds, then pour into a tall glass filled with ice. Top up with champagne and decorate with a mint leaf and a strawberry. Serve with straws.

Lovelight

1 ms brandy
1 ms passionfruit nectar
½ ms green Chartreuse
2 ice cubes

Blend all the ingredients together on slow speed for 10 seconds, then pour into a cocktail glass.

Mocha Flip

1 ms Bols Coffee Liqueur
1 egg yolk
1 tablespoon cream
2 ice cubes

Blend all the ingredients together on slow speed for 10 seconds, then pour into a cocktail glass. Grate nutmeg on top.

Ninety Park Lane

1 ms vodka
2 ms orange juice
½ ms Bols green Crème de Menthe
1 egg white
2 ice cubes

Blend together all except the crème de menthe on slow speed for 15 seconds, then pour into a medium-size goblet over a little crushed ice. Splash in the crème de menthe.

Paradise

1 ms gin
1 ms Bols Apricot Brandy
1 ms orange juice
2 ice cubes

Blend all the ingredients together on slow speed for 10 seconds, then pour into a cocktail glass.

Peach Paradise

1 ms gin
½ ms Bols Peach Brandy
½ ms orange juice
flesh of quarter peach
3 ice cubes

Blend all the ingredients together on slow speed for 15 seconds, then pour into a medium-size glass. Decorate with a slice of peach.

Perfect Love

1 ms vodka
½ ms Bols Parfait Amour
½ ms Bols Maraschino
1 scoop crushed ice

Blend all the ingredients together on slow speed for 15 seconds, then pour into a medium-size glass filled with ice.

Samurai

1 ms gin
1 ms passionfruit nectar
¼ ms Bols Blue Curacao
4 diced melon cubes
1 scoop crushed ice

Blend together all except the blue curacao on slow speed for 10 seconds, then pour into a tall glass filled with crushed ice. Splash blue curacao so it trickles down through the drink.

Straw Hat

1 ms gin
½ ms Midori melon liqueur
1 ms mango nectar
1 ms grapefruit juice
1 egg white
3 ice cubes

Blend all the ingredients together on slow speed for 15 seconds, then pour into a medium-size glass. Decorate with a slice of orange and a green cocktail cherry.

Tango

1½ ms Mandarine Napoleon
½ ms Bols Kirsch
pulp of half mango
1 scoop crushed ice

Blend all the ingredients together on slow speed for 15 seconds, then pour into a medium-size glass.

Tequila Fizz

1 ms tequila
1 ms grenadine
ginger ale
1 scoop crushed ice

Blend the tequila, grenadine and 3 measures of ginger ale with ice on slow speed for 10 seconds, then pour into a tall glass. Top up with more ginger ale and serve with straws.

Toasted Almond

2 ms Amaretto di Saronno
2 ms cream

Pour the amaretto into a small glass and float the cream on top.

White Knight

1 ms Malibu coconut liqueur
½ ms Drambuie
2 ms pineapple juice
2 ice cubes

Blend all the ingredients together on slow speed for 10 seconds, then pour into a medium-size glass.

Champagne Drinks

Alfonso

1 ms Dubonnet
2 dashes Angostura bitters
1 lump of sugar
champagne

Put two dashes of Angostura onto the sugar lump, then place in a champagne glass and add Dubonnet. Top with chilled champagne and place a twist of lemon peel on top.

Bellini

(Illustrated right)

2 ms Bols Peach Brandy
1 ms fresh lemon juice
1 peach
champagne

Blend together all except the champagne on slow speed for 15 seconds, then pour between champagne glasses, 1 oz/30 ml in each, and top up with cold champagne.

Black Velvet

Guinness
champagne

Half fill a small silver tankard or a champagne glass with Guinness, then slowly pour chilled champagne on top.

Camp Champ

1 ms Campari
1 ms orange juice
champagne
1 scoop crushed ice

Blend together all except the champagne on slow speed for 10 seconds, then pour into a tall glass. Add more crushed ice and top up with champagne. Decorate with an orange slice and a red cocktail cherry.

Left to right: *Lady Luisa, Kismet, Golden Year, Bellini, Mimosa, Singapore Fizz, Champagne Julep, Sea Serpent*

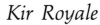

Champagne Julep

(Illustrated on pages 106–107)

1 ms Jack Daniels
3 sprigs of mint
1 sugar lump
champagne

Prepare in an old-fashioned glass, crushing the mint and sugar together with half of the Jack Daniels until it becomes paste.

Add the remainder of the Jack Daniels and pour the mixture into a champagne tulip glass. Top up with cold champagne.

Golden Year

(Illustrated on pages 106–107)

½ ms golden rum
½ ms Nassau Orange liqueur
champagne

Pour the rum and orange liqueur into a champagne glass and top up with cold champagne. Decorate with a quarter of orange and a red cocktail cherry.

Happy Hollander

¼ ms Bols Maraschino
½ ms mango nectar
¼ mango flesh
1 dash fresh lemon juice
1 dash sugar syrup
champagne

Blend together all except the champagne on slow speed for 10 seconds, then pour into a champagne glass. Top up with cold champagne.

Kir Royale

½ ms crème de cassis
champagne

Pour the creme de cassis into a champagne glass and top up with cold champagne.

Kismet

(Illustrated on pages 106–107)

1 ms gin
¼ ms Bols Gold Liqueur
1 dash fresh lemon juice
½ teaspoon ground ginger
3 cubes diced melon
champagne

Blend together all except the champagne on slow speed for 10 seconds, then pour into a tall glass filled with ice. Top up with cold champagne.

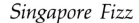

Lady Luisa

(Illustrated on pages 106–107)

1 ms calvados
1 ms pear nectar
3 cubes diced pear
champagne

Blend together all except the champagne on slow speed for 10 seconds, then pour into a flute glass. Top up with cold champagne.

Mimosa

(Illustrated on pages 106–107)

1 ms orange juice
½ ms Bols Dry Orange Curacao
champagne

Pour the orange juice and liqueur into a tulip or flute-type glass, then top up with cold champagne.

Rocky Gibraltar

¼ ms Bols green Crème de Menthe
champagne
1 in / 2.5 cm cucumber flesh

Blend the crème de menthe and cucumber flesh with 2 measures of champagne on slow speed for 10 seconds, then pour into a tall glass filled with ice. Top up with more champagne and drop in a slither of cucumber rind.

Sea Serpent

(Illustrated on pages 106–107)

¼ ms Bols green Crème de Menthe
champagne

Pour the crème de menthe into a champagne flute and top up with cold champagne. Drop in a slither of cucumber rind about 6 in / 15 cm long.

Singapore Fizz

(Illustrated on pages 106–107)

1 ms gin
½ ms Bols Cherry Brandy
½ ms fresh lemon juice
2 dashes sugar syrup
1 scoop crushed ice
champagne

Blend together all except the champagne on slow speed for 7 seconds, then pour into a tall glass and top up with champagne. A little more crushed ice may be a good idea. Decorate with a slice of lemon and a red cocktail cherry.

Southern Silk

1 ms gin
1 ms cream
½ ms Bols Dry Orange Curacao
2 dashes sugar syrup
1 scoop crushed ice
champagne

Blend together all except the champagne on fast speed for 10 seconds, then pour into a tall glass and top up with chilled champagne.

Coffee Drinks

Coffee Break

(Illustrated below)

1 ms light rum
½ ms Malibu coconut liqueur
½ ms Bols Coffee Liqueur
3 diced pineapple cubes
1 teaspoon instant coffee
1 scoop crushed ice

Blend all the ingredients together on slow speed until smooth, then pour into a medium-size glass. Decorate with crushed pineapple.

Irish Coffee

(Illustrated below)

1 ms Irish whiskey
2 teaspoons Demerara sugar
coffee
cream

Blend the sugar and the whiskey in a medium-size goblet, then pour in very hot black coffee. Stir until the sugar is completely dissolved, then pour cream over the back of a warm spoon so that it floats on top.

Many other spirits and liqueurs blend very well with coffee and cream.

Moonlight

1 ms Mandarine Napoleon
½ ms brandy
2 teaspoons Demerara sugar
coffee
cream

Mix the sugar and the Mandarine liqueur in a medium-size goblet, then pour in very hot black coffee. Stir until the sugar is completely dissolved. Mix the brandy with the cream and pour over the back of a warm spoon so that it floats on top.

Mulatta

1 ms dark rum
2 ms cold coffee
1 scoop vanilla ice cream
cream

Blend together all except the cream on slow speed for 10 seconds, then pour into a medium-size glass and float cream on top.

Cognac, Irish Coffee, Coffee Break

Nassau Express

1 ms Nassau Orange liqueur
½ ms brandy
1 scoop coffee ice cream
2 ice cubes

Blend all the ingredients together on slow speed for 10 seconds, then pour into a small glass and dust with instant coffee.

Nine Carat

1 ms dark rum
½ ms Bols Gold Liqueur
3 ms cold coffee
1 scoop vanilla ice cream
2 ice cubes

Blend the rum, coffee and ice cubes on fast speed for 7 seconds, then pour into a sundae glass and drop in a ball of ice cream. Splash Gold Liqueur on top and serve with straws.

Ready-to-Wear

1 ms vodka
½ ms Bols Dry Orange Curacao
1 ms cold coffee
1 scoop crushed ice

Blend all the ingredients together on fast speed for 5 seconds, then pour into a medium-size glass.

Frappés

A frappé is usually any liqueur or spirit simply poured into a small glass over crushed ice. It is not unusual to mix two or more liqueurs together, so below are listed some of the popular frappés.

Café Royal Frappé

1 ms brandy
1 ms cold coffee

Shake the ingredients with ice and strain into a small goblet filled with crushed ice. Serve with short straws.

Harlequin Frappé

1 ms vodka
1 ms Bols Dry Orange Curacao
1 ms Bols brown Crème de Cacao

Pour into a small straight-sided glass over crushed ice in order listed.

Mother-of-Pearl

1 ms gin
1 ms Bols Anisette

Pour in any order into a small glass filled with crushed ice. Serve with straws.

Sticky Green

(Illustrated on page 103)

2 ms Bols green Crème de Menthe

Pour into a small glass filled with crushed ice. Serve with short straws.

Traffic Light

1 ms Bols green Crème de Menthe
1 ms Bols Cherry Brandy
1 ms Bols Dry Orange Curacao

Pour into a small straight-sided glass over crushed ice in order listed.

WHISKY: *forever amber*

Scottish for Water

'Whisky and freedom gang together' said Robbie Burns, and it is true that the Scots have so jealously defended their right to distil whisky that the spirit has become inextricably linked with the nation's history. The Scots took to distilling in the Middle Ages, when it was probably introduced by missionary monks from Ireland, and referred to the drink as *uisge beathe*, the Gaelic for 'water of life'. The English, however, were unable to manage the pronunciation and the closest they could say to *uisge* was 'whisky'.

Many highlanders and homesteaders had their own stills and production became so widespread that by 1643 the Scottish Parliament saw whisky as an excellent source of revenue. So began the long battle between the illegal whisky distiller and the excise man. Many Scots were happy enough to aid the 'home' distiller as he was a source of cheap whisky and the excise man represented a remote and demanding government, so the smuggler was tacitly acknowledged as a member of the local community. Women would light washing fires to hide the smoke from illegal stills, casks were hidden in churches and smugglers' wives carried containers of whisky under their skirts and delivered door to door. By 1823 the battle had reached the proportions of a national sport and 14,000 illegal stills were confiscated in that year. Eventually a reasonable level of taxation encouraged the growth of a respectable distilling industry, and with the use of the newly invented continuous still, quality whisky could be produced cheaply and in quantity.

Originally whisky was made from malted barley which is distilled in batches in a pot still. However, the continuous still could provide a constant supply of spirit distilled from maize. The availability of these cheaper grain whiskies introduced a new dimension to the business as it was possible to blend the malt and grain spirits together. This, combined with the new idea of selling the beverage in glass bottles, meant that a consistent flavour could be maintained and the product could be 'exported' to England, so that by the turn of the 20th century, whisky was big business.

Spirit of America

The settlers of North America in colonial times were great rum drinkers, as it could be readily obtained from the West Indies. Some of the larger estates had their own stills, but with imported spirits readily available there was little need for much locally distilled liquor. These circumstances altered in 1775 when the American War of Independence began and the British threw a naval blockade around the coast, cutting off supplies. So, if the settlers were to have enough liquor, it had to be produced within their own borders. Spirit was used for medicinal purposes, being administered before all operations, at childbirth and the like, so was much in demand by doctors, veterinarians, ministers and soldiers.

Enterprising Scots and Irish settlers set up distilleries to produce liquor for commercial purposes – one such entrepreneur was Reverend Elijah Craig whose still was in Georgetown, Bourbon County, Kentucky. His distillery was beside a limestone creek with a plentiful supply of pure clean water and he began producing a goodly drop of corn liquor so tasty that customers began asking for it by name – Kentucky Bourbon Whiskey. Gradually the fame of his drink spread and 'Bourbon' came to mean any superior liquor until eventually the product itself became known as Bourbon.

High Voltage Specials

Alaska

1 ms gin
1 ms Yellow Chartreuse
2 ice cubes

Blend all the ingredients together on slow speed for 10 seconds, then pour into a cocktail glass.

Alligator

1 ms Jack Daniels
½ ms Bols Blue Curacao
½ ms fresh lemon juice
1 dash egg white
2 ice cubes

Blend all the ingredients together on slow speed for 10 seconds, then pour into a cocktail glass and decorate with a red cocktail cherry.

Blackjack

1 ms Jack Daniels
½ ms dry vermouth
2 dashes crème de cassis
1 scoop crushed ice

Blend all the ingredients together on slow speed for 7 seconds, then pour into a medium-size glass.

Bleu-Do-It

(Illustrated right)

1 ms gin
1 ms vodka
1 ms tequila
1 ms Bols Blue Curacao
1 ms fresh lemon juice
2 dashes egg white
soda water

Blend together all except the soda water on fast speed for 5 seconds, then pour into a tall glass filled with ice. Top up with soda and decorate with slices of lemon and a green cocktail cherry.

Blue Shark

(Illustrated on pages 118–119)

1 ms tequila
1 ms vodka
1 ms Bols Blue Curacao
3 ice cubes

Blend all the ingredients together on slow speed for 10 seconds, then pour into a cocktail glass filled with ice.

Brave Bull

1 ms tequila
1 ms Kahlua
2 ice cubes

Blend all the ingredients together on fast speed for 10 seconds, then pour into a medium-size glass filled with ice.

Left to right: *Cobra, Hunting Pink, Bleu-Do-It, Ghosthunter, Dragon Slayer*

Chocolate Bomber

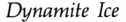

(Illustrated on pages 118–119)

1 ms dark rum
1 ms Bols Chocolate Mint
dash cream
dash egg white
3 ice cubes

Blend all the ingredients together on slow speed for 10 seconds, then pour into a tall glass filled with ice and splash a little dark rum on top. Dust with chocolate.

Cobra

(Illustrated on page 115)

1 ms Southern Comfort
½ ms Bols Parfait Amour
½ ms bourbon
3 ice cubes

Blend all the ingredients together on slow speed for 10 seconds, then pour into a medium-size glass filled with crushed ice.

Dragon Slayer

1 ms gin
1 ms Bols Cherry Brandy
½ ms Bols Kirsch
4 maraschino cherries
2 ice cubes

Blend all the ingredients together on slow speed for 10 seconds, then pour into a medium-size glass. Decorate with a slice of lemon and a red cocktail cherry.

Dynamite Ice

(Illustrated on pages 118–119)

1 ms Campari
1 ms Bols Cherry Brandy
1 ms gin
cream
2 ice cubes

Blend together all except the cream on slow speed for 10 seconds, then pour into a medium-size glass filled with crushed ice. Pour cream on top. Decorate with two blue cocktail cherries.

French Connection

1 ms brandy
1 ms amaretto
2 ice cubes

Blend all the ingredients together on slow speed for 10 seconds, then pour into a cocktail glass or into a medium-size glass filled with ice.

Fort Knox

1 ms brandy
½ ms Galliano
½ ms Bols Gold Liqueur
½ ms orange juice
2 ice cubes

Blend all the ingredients together on slow speed for 10 seconds, then pour into a cocktail glass.

Firecracker

1 ms dark rum
½ ms sambuca
½ ms brandy
2 pineapple cubes
2 ice cubes

Blend together all except the brandy on slow speed for 15 seconds, then pour into a cocktail or sherry glass. Float the warmed brandy on top and ignite.

Ghosthunter

(Illustrated on page 115)

1 ms Jack Daniels
1 ms Southern Comfort
2 ice cubes

Blend all the ingredients together on slow speed for 10 seconds, then pour into a medium-size glass filled with ice.

Godfather

1 ms bourbon
1 ms amaretto
2 ice cubes

Blend all the ingredients together on slow speed for 10 seconds, then pour into a medium-size glass filled with ice.

Green Spider

2 ms vodka
1 ms Bols green Crème de Menthe
2 ice cubes

Blend all the ingredients together on slow speed for 10 seconds, then pour into a medium-size glass filled with ice.

Hunting Pink

(Illustrated on page 115)

1 ms tequila
½ ms sambuca
½ ms Campari
1 dash egg white
2 strawberries
2 ice cubes

Blend all the ingredients together on slow speed for 15 seconds, then pour into a medium-size glass filled with ice.

Jack Dempsey

2 ms calvados
1 ms gin
2 dashes Bols Anisette
1 dash grenadine
1 scoop crushed ice

Blend all the ingredients together on slow speed for 10 seconds, then pour into a medium-size glass. Decorate with a strawberry.

Jade Lady

(Illustrated on pages 118–119)

1 ms light rum
1 ms gin
½ ms Bols green Creme de Menthe
½ ms sugar syrup
dash lemon juice
3 ice cubes

Blend all the ingredients together on slow speed for 10 seconds, then pour into a flute glass filled with ice.

Left to right: *Chocolate Bomber, Jade Lady, Rusty Nail, Dynamite Ice, Blue Shark, Silver Stream*

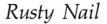

Kentucky Colonel

1½ ms bourbon
½ ms Bénédictine
2 ice cubes

Blend all the ingredients together on slow speed for 10 seconds, then pour into a cocktail glass. Add a twist of lemon.

Mist

Blend 1 measure of any spirit or liqueur with half a scoop of crushed ice on slow speed for 10 seconds, then pour over crushed ice in an old-fashioned glass. Add a twist of lemon.

Piranha

1 ms vodka
1 ms Bols brown Crème de Cacao
2 ice cubes

Blend all the ingredients together on slow speed for 10 seconds, then pour into a cocktail glass.

Rasputin's Revenge

1 ms vodka
1 ms Bols Blue Curacao
2 ice cubes

Blend all the ingredients together on slow speed for 10 seconds, then pour into a cocktail glass.

Rusty Nail

(Illustrated on pages 118–119)

1 ms Scotch whisky
1 ms Drambuie
2 ice cubes

Blend all the ingredients together on slow speed for 10 seconds, then pour into a medium-size glass filled with ice. Add a twist of lemon.

Silver Bullet

1 ms vodka
1 ms Bols Kummel
2 ice cubes

Blend all the ingredients together on slow speed for 10 seconds, then pour into a cocktail glass or into a medium-size glass filled with ice.

Silver Streak

1 ms gin
1 ms Bols Kummel
2 ice cubes

Blend all the ingredients together on slow speed for 10 seconds, then pour into a cocktail glass or into a medium-size glass filled with ice.

Silver Stream

(Illustrated on pages 118–119)

1 ms vodka
1 ms light rum
½ ms gin
dash lime juice
dash sugar syrup
3 ice cubes

Blend all the ingredients together on slow speed for 10 seconds, then pour into a flute glass filled with ice. Serve with a stirrer.

Southern Teul

1 ms tequila
1 ms Southern Comfort
2 ice cubes

Blend all the ingredients together on slow speed for 10 seconds, then pour into a cocktail glass.

Surfside

1 ms light rum
1 ms Southern Comfort
1 ms Bols Crème de Banane
1 ms Bols Peach Brandy
1 ms orange juice
2 dashes grenadine
8 ice cubes

Blend all the ingredients together on fast speed for 7 seconds, then strain into a tall glass or coconut shell. Decorate with a slice of orange and red cocktail cherries. Serve with a straw.

Spark Plug

1 ms gin
1 ms Cointreau
1 ms Bols Kummel
2 ice cubes

Blend all the ingredients together on slow speed for 10 seconds, then pour into a cocktail glass.

The Rocket

1 ms akvavit
1 ms Bols Kummel
1 scoop crushed ice

Blend all the ingredients together on fast speed for 7 seconds, then pour into a medium-size glass.

Tokyo Joe

1 ms vodka
½ ms Midori melon liqueur
2 ice cubes

Blend all the ingredients together on slow speed for 10 seconds, then pour into a cocktail glass or into a medium-size glass filled with ice.

Waikiki

2 ms Jack Daniels
1 ms Bols Dry Orange Curacao
½ ms fresh lemon juice
1 dash grenadine
2 ice cubes

Blend all the ingredients together on slow speed for 10 seconds, then pour into a medium-size glass filled with ice. Add a twist of lemon.

Index